Christian and Islamic Spirituality

Sharing a Journey

Paulist Press ◊ New York ◊ Mahwah, N.J.

ACKNOWLEDGMENTS

The Publisher gratefully acknowledges use of material from *The Collected Works of St. John of the Cross* translated by Kieran Kavanaugh and Otilio Rodriguez © 1979 by Washington Province of Discalced Carmelites. ICS Publications 2131 Lincoln Road, N.E. Washington, D.C. 20002 U.S.A.; quotations from *Open Secret: Version of Rumi,* translated by J. Moyne and C. Barks, copyright © 1984 by Threshold Books, RD 4 Box 600, Putney, Vermont 05346.

Scripture quotations are from the Revised Standard Version of the Bible, copyright © 1946, 1952, 1971 by the Division of Christian Education of the National Council of the Churches of Christ in the USA.

Library of Congress Cataloging-in-Publication Data

Jaoudi, Maria.
    Christian and Islamic spirituality: sharing a journey / Maria
    Jaoudi. p. cm.
    Includes bibliographical references and index.
    ISBN 0-8091-3426-8 (pbk.)
    1. Sufism—Relations—Catholic Church. 2. Catholic Church—
Relations—Sufism. 3. Spirituality—Catholic Church. 4. Sufism—
Doctrines. 5. Catholic Church—Doctrines. I. Title.
    BP189.3.J37 1993
    248—dc20   93-25368
                                                                CIP

Published by Paulist Press
997 Macarthur Boulevard
Mahwah, New Jersey 07430

Printed and bound in the
United States of America

Contents

To My Mother,
My First Spiritual Teacher

Introduction

This book is an attempt to elaborate on the spiritual affinity between the traditions of Christianity and Islam. With Judaism, Christianity and Islam share the same monotheistic God and basic mythology of the Hebrew scriptures. Since Christianity and Islam also share in many of the beliefs of the New Testament, this book hopes to demonstrate the similarities between the two traditions.

Structurally, I have endeavored to base the chapters on the spiritual journey itself, the classical mystical stages of purification, transformation, and finally, union with God. Each chapter centers on the insights of saints and theologians from both traditions. And, since we are in the throes of a global environmental crisis, it seemed of the utmost importance to conclude the book with a God-centered ecology, which has been a component of both these world views for centuries.

Perhaps it is obvious to point to the fact that Islam and Christianity share so much spiritually, but with all the historical misunderstandings, it is hoped that a renewed effort emphasizing points of convergence and overlap, will help to bring about world peace.

I have written this book remembering a childhood that bridged two religious experiences in Africa, Europe, and the Middle East. I can vividly remember the call of the muezzin at dusk as the swallows circled the minarets in different Muslim towns, and the smell of candles and the distinctive hush of a medieval Catholic chapel in Paris. These are some of the deep, loved memories.

From these experiences grew the intimate knowledge of how beautiful and meaningful each tradition is in and of itself. There is room in our hearts and on the planet for both traditions. We, in fact, need both. That little girl knew it two decades ago, and it is her vision which has not aged, and for which there is still hope.

1

The Way of Love

For a Christian or a Muslim who really lives his or her tradition, there exists a very important experience in common, namely, a profound inner knowing that God is love. The Christian saints and the Sufi mystics have called God guide, protector, creator, friend, beloved. In other words, God is the way to learn about love, because the essential nature of divinity is substantive mercy. The guide who calls us into full actualization, the protector preserving us from unnecessary harm, the creator who shares the immanence of divinity through our body-selves and the earth-body, the friend listening, always listening, and the beloved loving us just as we are; these are all dimensions of God's personal care for us as individuals.

Psychology tells us that it is only when we recognize our own worth, our own likeableness, that we are then led to believe in our potential lovableness to another. In the spirituality of Islam and Christianity, a gradual recognition of one's own sense of worth is experienced because of having allowed God to truly enter the heart and transform the wounds every human being develops in one form or another throughout life.

Teresa of Avila in sixteenth-century Christian Spain, and Rabi'a al-Adawiyya in the eighth century living in what today is modern Iraq, are examples of women who obviously did not have the psychological training of a C. G. Jung or Alice Miller, but Teresa and Rabi'a did apprehend intuitively what contemporary psychology would regard as a profound understanding of the self. Teresa and Rabi'a journeyed into the reality of healing love within their own hearts, and were able to universalize their own personal experience into a path that could guide others. "The Friend who lives in my house/ Is the lover of my Heart,"[1] declares Rabi'a. The house of the self is a dwelling place in which the beloved friend heals and teaches her heart all about herself! Rabi'a is describing the intimate reality of not only recognizing that God lives within the self, but allowing God to function freely in the loving form and expression of beloved and friend. This relationship is described by Jesus in John's gospel as the home that Christ will create within, the dwelling which draws us closer to knowing we have been called as friends, not as servants.

There have been theologians in both Islam and Christianity who have preferred, unfortunately, to regard themselves and the rest of us as slaves, rather than friends of God. In keeping with an informed sociological approach regarding the self as individuated being, worthy spiritually and socially of a democratically-oriented deity, oppressing neither female nor male, we shall focus on the Qur'anic and New Testament ideals of freedom, equality, and the dignity of our immanent status as just and loving people.

How we view ourselves through God's eyes, directly affects how we embody the sacred personally and socially. If we view ourselves in the more mystical mode of beloved, we will not find it necessary to regard either ourselves or others as higher or lower, master or slave. Our deepest authority will be, instead, love grounded in truth and caring. Therein, even our God hopes for our liberation with a mercy freely given and brimming with divine generosity. "A new commandment I give to you, that you love one another; even as I have loved you, that you also love one another."[2]

The way of love begins with personally working through one's own psychological healing, continues in reaching the center of genuinely experiencing one's lovableness, and finally, blossoms forth in a joyous giving to others overflowing with that divine mercy from which one has immeasurably drunk. "Could one conceal a love that is so strong and just that it always increases and sees no reason to stop since its foundation is made from the cement of being repaid by another love?"[3]

Why the Means Is the Same as the End

The two founders of Islam and Christianity, Muhammad and Jesus, made no separation either in their teachings or in their actions, in terms of means-end relationship. How you achieved your goal, was just as important as the goal itself. Therefore, if the goal of life is union with God, and then, loving neighbor, how we journey toward God is as much an aspect of spiritual achievement and attainment as oneness with God. Both Muhammad and Jesus explain that the first commandment is first for a reason:

> You shall love the Lord your God with all your heart, and with all your soul, and with all you mind. This is the great and first commandment. And the second is like it, you shall love your neighbor as yourself. On these two commandments depend all the law and the prophets.[4]

Both traditions declare that it is not enough to make an external commitment to God; one must love with the whole of one's being—with all one's heart, soul, and mind. This is the means to God: *lā ilāha illā'l-'ishq*, "there is no deity save Love."[5] The point is that the emphasis should be on working with God and through God's love, rather than holding God "out there," as an external idol. Islam is as clear as Christianity; the true believer is the one who lives lovingly, not in a sentimental way, but through care and sacrifice, in city or desert, in community or alone. Idolatry takes many forms; two of the more obvious externalize worshiping God either through duty or ritualistic enactment. If we have not love first, the duty or ritual will lose its essential meaning. If we maintain a loving attitude at the core of our activities, God is then moving through our being in whatever we may say or do. The duty is done with joy, the ritual comes alive with devotional meaning.

Islam speaks of "realized knowledge," a knowing that is awake and ready to act: "All power, all activity is ours/ only so much as GOD is us."[6] One would not therefore, create a dualism between, for example, how one cooked a meal, or drove on the highway, from ways of being God-bearers. Jesus spoke of this truth as, whatever you do to the least of these, you do to me. The rights of the least go back in the west to Aristotelian ethics, whereby one's character is revealed through how one makes large decisions, or performs small actions. The immanence of God is revealed through the means too often forgotten; how one looks at a tree (noble in itself, or merely to be chopped down for economic profit), listens to a child, regards the workplace (a job I love and find fulfillment within, or merely a means for survival), eats, walks, breathes (Thomas Merton spoke of the sage as so integrated that breathing came through the toes). When dimensions of the Self center on a consciousness of the sacred, such a consciousness permeates the self ontologically. The actions one performs, then, reveal the extent to which the divine has become one's own self and ultimate purpose.

As the lover in the beloved
Each lived in the other,
And the Love that unites them
Is one with them.[7]

The transcendent God becomes immanent through the individual's embodied consciousness. When whatever I do becomes a dimension and revelation of the holy, a living in the eternal now, I have become one with the Beloved, and have entered a state of being in which the means-end relationship is joined through what St. John of the Cross calls "loving awareness."

Centering on the Beloved

Loving awareness manifests an integrated personhood unifying love, consciousness, and guidance through discernment. Discernment is that unique quality of spiritual wakefulness which Christianity and Islam define as learning to decipher, discern, God's will in situational ethics, situations of the heart, in the innermost center of one's being where the voice of God is lucid and uncompromisingly good. To truly embody love, consciousness, and oneness with God, is to have gained a certain degree of discerning knowledge enabling one to perceive the difference between needs and wants. It is that same discerning knowledge that grows qualitatively to the degree one is centered in God, and therein aware of God's will, the perspective in union with one's deepest self and truest aspirations. The more in touch we are with what we really need, the less tempted we will be by unnecessary wants which may take the form of distractions, unhealed habits or dependencies. Put simply, whatever leads us away from the first commandment, from God first, places wants above needs, which may lead to a glorification of the false ego.

Centering on the beloved, then, has a multipurposed criterion helping the individual person become healthy on the physical, psychological, social and, of course, spiritual levels. If I choose junk food for lunch, rather than a hearty sandwich, something is amiss with my criteria for physical well-being. When it comes to criteria for all one's needs, Christianity and Islam agree that if one's perspective is solidly grounded in transcendent awareness, one becomes cognizant of God's immanence as well. "God is the Light of Heaven and Earth!"[8]

God's light is visible to those who have come in contact with the source of all light. "Once the seeker has arrived at this point, the heart is filled with brilliant light and over-whelming insights, so that a portion of the Lord's indescrib-able majesty and grandeur and some of the marvels of the worlds of God's power and wisdom become manifest."[9] Indeed, the luminous glory of the creator is present through new eyes, because the vision one now possesses is rooted in loving awareness. By centering on the beloved, the light which so often signifies the numinous, becomes a part of my everyday world. I will see and experience the same world, the same people, animals, sky, and earth, but I will view them differently through the eyes of transformed glory.

> My beloved speaks and says to me:
> "Arise, my love . . .
> The flowers appear on earth,
>   the time of singing has come,
> and the voice of the turtledove
>   is heard in the land.

The fig tree puts forth its figs,
and the vines are in blossom;
they give forth fragrance."[10]

When the beloved speaks, love is revealed and reality is experienced from the transcendent perspective. This puts a unique stamp on every aspect of reality, including how one will now comprehend suffering and death, since the standard is not simply a finite one, but *sub species eternitatus*. And under the aspect of eternity, the finite world becomes imbued with values that dignify and uplift all of life.

Mircea Eliade in the book *The Sacred and the Profane,* observes that when the transcendent perspective is lost, all that had been sacred and filled with dignity and meaning, is profaned through secularization.[11] Out of fear, one of the severest reactions that Christianity and Islam have had to secularization, is to fall into fundamentalism. Instead of attempting to integrate the "sacred" benefits of technology and modernization, a total reversal is called for by fundamentalism, which denies most of the positive steps humanity has taken in the last several centuries toward the elimination of poverty, medical improvements, and education for people other than the monied elite. Certain Islamic sects have stated that the godless noise and haste of the west demonstrates the evils of modern society. They certainly have a point as anyone who has had to contend with the likes of blasting radios, airplanes overhead, or the frantic speed in so many normal daily transactions can testify. Many Christians, too, have fled into fundamentalist groups where, for example, women do not wear slacks or work outside the home, as a reaction to the destruction of the family and family values that have occurred in many secularized cultures. They do have a point, since the divorce rate has skyrocketed, and latchkey children are not what one would hope childhood would be about. Fundamentalist groups seem to be looking for refuge in antiquated cultural norms which, in effect, is like asking people to wear cloaks and sandals because that is what Jesus and Muhammad certainly wore in the desert.

What I would like to suggest in terms of a valid spirituality, is that we be not afraid of secularization or modernity, even to the degree of being willing to scrutinize the ramifications both positive and negative on our belief systems. Television can be violent and sexually exploitive, but it can also be a means for seeing the best plays and learning about topics one would usually have no exposure to: whether God's tigers in India, how the human brain functions, or the importance of dogs and cats in the lives of shut-ins and the elderly.

Rumi declared: "Without God's countenance, paradise for me is hateful hell."[12] There is no doubt that much of what technocratic society has created is "godless," reflecting meaninglessness, and therefore is like a kind of hell. But is it not possible to see the beloved's countenance in the beauty of irrigation, a successful operation, or in a young girl's aspirations to be whatever the Creator has given her the potential to be?

Christian Love

"And the Word became flesh and dwelt among us, full of grace and truth."[13] There is no greater nor profounder way of expressing God's love than the incarnation. That ultimate Being would become flesh and dwell with us; touch, eat, heal, have friends, and voluntarily suffer and die for every person who seeks the path of union with

God—one can only stand in awe before the stark beauty of the cross, just as the Hindu, Mahatma Gandhi did, weeping at the sight of God bleeding when the Mahatma visited the Sistine chapel. All of Christian love, all the centuries of Christian mysticism, both western and eastern, center on the sacrifice and resurrection of the love embodied in Jesus the Christ. *Da amantem et scit quod dico:* "Bring me a lover: that one will understand what I am saying (Saint Augustine)."

One of the best approaches to learn about Christian love, is to read John's gospel, especially the last supper discourse, the crucifixion, and finally, Christ resurrected preparing food for the disciples calling to them: "Come and have breakfast."[14] Christ has crossed the barrier of death, returning in glory. He calls to those he has loved so deeply in life, and yet does not preach to them, but instead, tenderly prepares for them an everyday meal. The entire structure of theology rests on the fact that the glorified one teaches through such humble actions.

> O righteous Father, the world has not known thee, but I have known thee; and these know that thou has sent me. I made known to them thy name, and I will make it known, that the love with which thou hast loved me may be in them, and I in them.[15]

Jesus tells us that God is not just protector or creator, but intimate parent, "Abba," one whom we can freely communicate with in joy and in sorrow, with love or anger, because God's presence is now in us as God is in Jesus. That is the message and mission of Jesus; to bring each person into a relational union with God.

The emphasis in Christianity on the historical Jesus is directly linked to the belief in the Holy Spirit. The Spirit teaches each of us how to be who we are in a Christ-like way. It is not enough to imitate Christ; it is more important, in the words of Catherine of Siena, to be "another Christ." What this means is that the Spirit guides us in the internal journey, and leads us in the world through discernment and truth, bringing the transforming light to shatter darkness. Christians believe that God has created every woman and man to image the divine in a unique form distinctly suited and created for that person's Christ-like capacity. "For love! You, God, became human and we have been made divine!"[16] Jesus is the way and the door, the teacher and guide, and especially, in terms of spirituality, the beloved who speaks to us revealing the hidden face within, our own face as reflected in the divine heart.

Karl Rahner stated that Jesus is God's heart made flesh; to understand and study the person of Jesus is to comprehend the very pulse of divinity. Jesus is the Word of God, articulating the nature of the Christ through the beatitudes, through the miracles of healing and feeding the hungry, through his profound friendships and sacrificial fearlessness. If we follow in the steps of Jesus, the Christ-potential is released within us, and we become a new creation alive to the word spoken to us within and in every situation of daily life. "If you travel along this delightful straight way which is a lightsome truth, holding the key of obedience, you will pass through the world's darkness without stumbling. And in the end you will unlock heaven with the Word's key."[17]

Islamic Love

Muhammad, the founder of Islam, was born in 570 C.E. in Mecca. Orphaned at a tender age, Muhammad would never forget the experience of being marginalized. His sympathy toward orphans, widows, and poor folk, later led him to battle the established elite of wealthy clan leaders. Raised by an uncle, Muhammad married his employer, Khadija, who was older than he. They had six children, but only four daughters survived.

Muhammad was fond of solitary prayer practised in the abandoned desert hills. At a certain point in his meditations, he began to receive divine revelations from Allah (God) given through the angel Gabriel. These revelations became the Islamic Qur'an, "The Book," which is read by every Muslim devotedly and frequently. Over the centuries, neither western scholars, nor Islamic theologians, have been able to find a reason why Muhammad, an illiterate caravan merchant, could have conceived single-handedly the sublime and elegant classical Arabic which make up the *suras* (chapters) of the Qur'an. It is therefore believed, as part of the Islamic creed, that Muhammad was a direct instrument, or mouthpiece, for God's final revelation to the Judeo-Christian tradition: "There is no God but Allah, and Muhammad is his prophet."

A shy man, Muhammad, like Plato's philosopher-king, did not want to become a public leader; rather he yearned for a quiet introspective life, worshiping God and meditating further on the truths he had so unexpectedly been given.

Nonetheless, the power of the Qur'anic message, together with his wife's and uncle's encouragement, led Muhammad into a position of leadership that was to conquer most of the Arab world and parts of Africa during the prophet's own lifetime. Muhammad would risk everything to create a community of "submitters to God"—Muslims. Known for his humility, sense of humor, and extraordinary military and political skills, Muhammad never claimed miraculous powers, always stressing his ordinariness in the face of an extraordinary message.

The Islamic conception of God as love is expressed in the first verse of Al-Qur'an: "In the name of God, the compassionate, the merciful (*Bismillah al-rahman al-rahim*)." God's mercy is greater than our imagining, and paradoxically, closer to us than our own jugular vein. The transcendence of God is evoked continuously in the Muslim world. Take, for example, the haunting voice of the muezzin calling the faithful to prayer. The singer's *allah akbar* (Greater is God) flows like a river of sincere praise over Islamic cities and villages from the balconies of the minarets which thrust into the sky. Full of emotion, and yet, emptying the moment of any other concern except that of concentrating on God's transcendence and compassionate will.

The mosque also demonstrates the totally transcendent nature of the divine because no images are allowed except for the "geometry of the spirit," calligraphy. And yet, the immanence of God is celebrated through the horizontal structure of the mosque itself, that hugs the earth with broad, magnificent buildings, turquoise and gold archways, rich embroidered rugs within, and lamps hanging like clear tears, reminding the faithful of God's infinite love pervading the mosque and all of life. The mosque does mirror both the transcendent emphasis of Islam, and Islam's intense this-worldiness.

Celibacy is discouraged; Muhammad himself believed that marriage was God's call to a more fulfilled life. One also aspires to financial success. One's family, work, and prayer are an interwoven endeavor to reveal the presence of God's mercy through spiritual growth and outreach. Each household gives alms comprising twenty percent of the family's income, and looks to help those who have encountered misfortune.

One's home is symbolic of the transcendent realm present on earth. Every home ideally should have a courtyard which, like heaven, is verdant, with perhaps a gentle fountain at the center, protected, quiet, always expressing God's alive and indefinable presence immanently.

Historically, it is important to remember, most of Islam's victories over other lands and religions have been through peaceful trade. Although bloody invaders brandishing swords is often what comes to mind for the westener when it comes to Islamic territorial victories, in actual fact, most nations that converted to Islam did so out of desire for Islamic values and to advance materially. Islam is a universalistic religion, the light "kindled from a blessed olive tree, which is neither of the East nor the West."[18] Along with trade, Islam's ability to relate to people of many races and cultures, poor and rich, has made it the world's fastest growing religion today. One out of every five people on the planet is Muslim. In the United States, for example, it is the converts to Islam, especially those from the city ghettos, who rid the projects of drug dealers, espouse education, and call for the renewal of family values. The universalistic message of Islam, the power of Allah's compassion, is evident in those nations that are taking care of their citizenry, imitating Muhammad's love of education and community.

A Muslim Lover: Rabi'a al-Adawiyya

Rabi'a was born in 717 C.E. according to Islamic hagiography. Most of the stories and poems we have about Rabi'a's life and work are tinged with mythos. She embodied an ideal of total devotion to God, but at the same time she appeals to modern women especially, because of her independent spirit and lucid intellect.

Rabi'a lived in what is now Iraq, and is considered one of the major saints of Islam, particularly of the Sufi tradition. Her early life was filled with tragedy: her family was poor, and when famine struck, both parents died. Rabi'a was sold into slavery, later to be freed by a generous master. According to legend, her master would awaken during the night and see Rabi'a at prayer suspended in mid-air, a miraculous lamp shining above her head illuminating the entire house.[19] Perhaps such a vision convinced Rabi'a's master of her saintliness, for he then freed her.

Having lived under the yoke of slavery, Rabi'a was to disdain any tie that might smack of humiliation. She was an early feminist simply because of who she was and how she chose to live. For the rest of her life (d. 801), she lived completely focused on God. Rabi'a meditated for extensive periods of time and developed specific spiritual exercises, ran her home, and taught those who came to her for guidance (often feeding them as well). She never married, and although famous in the latter part of her life, declined a continuous flow of marriage proposals, financial gifts, and even property.

It is believed that Rabi'a made the required Islamic pilgrimage to Mecca. One of her "teachings" centers on the meaning of her journey:

It took Ibrahim Ibn Adham fourteen years to reach the Kaaba in pilgrimage, because he said long prayers at every shrine along the way—but when he got there, there was no Kaaba to be seen. "What is this?" he asked himself. "Have I gone blind?"

"No," a Voice said, "you can't see the Kaaba because it has gone out to meet a woman." Burning with jealousy, Ibrahim ran toward the outskirts of Mecca till he ran into Rabi'a, who was just arriving. He turned around, and saw the Kaaba back in its usual place. Then he turned to Rabi'a.

"What's this craziness you've brought into the world, woman?" he demanded.

"It's not I who am the author of craziness," she replied, "but you. You were crazy enough to take fourteen years to get to the Kaaba with your ritual prayer, while I, with my inner prayer, am here already."[20]

The inner prayer Rabi'a espoused is that complete consciousness of God working from within outward. Being a true mystic and Sufi, Rabi'a had little respect for asceticism for asceticism's sake, and some of her acerbic remarks to the other sages of that era, such as Ibrahim Ibn Adham, can be attributed to lessons on the difference between Rabi'a's devotional love and the outward practices of fasting, vigils, saying "long prayers at every shrine" on the way to the Kaaba, that characterize superficial piety. Rabi'a's zeal is not unique in the history of religion; one has only to look at the life of Buddha or Jesus, both of whom condemned external asceticism: cleaning the outer cup, but leaving the inside of the cup dirty.

It is fascinating, however, to look at just how much of an ascetic Rabi'a was for all her condemnations of this purifying path. She did prove in her person the difference between the asceticism which is a path in itself, resulting in pride and separation from other beings, and that true asceticism which purifies the heart, bringing one closer to God through viewing the reflection of the sacred in the world within and without.

"True devotion is for God: not to desire heaven nor fear hell."[21] Rabi'a believed that even in the spiritual life there existed a temptation to turn away from the beloved either through desires that form unhealthy attachments, or, through fears that block the necessary trust existing in any genuine love relationship. Rabi'a, therefore, is known throughout the Muslim world as the model of the selfless lover who ceaselessly seeks God first, and thereby avoids any of temptation's pitfalls. To this day, one is complimented by being referred to as "another Rabi'a"—she who lived only for God, the second Mary.

Rabi'a is the herald of love mysticism in Sufism, her very clear prayer consisting of the words: "Thou art enough for me."[22] Rabi'a attained a unified God-consciousness in her life exemplifying that pragmatic holiness at-one with God. She was always available to people who sought for themselves a relationship of union with God. And, like our next saint, Francis of Assisi, she remained open to God's immanence in the created universe. No animal ran from Rabi'a, and when she would pray in the mountains, "all the animals, the deer and the wild asses, the goats and gazelles, came up to her, and gazed at her, and danced around her."[23]

A Christian Lover: Francis of Assisi

Francis was born in 1181 C.E. in Assisi, the son of a successful merchant. A popular youth, Francis spent much of his early life singing and entertaining his friends. His conversion was gradual. Eventually the joyfulness of his youth was to create the unique flavor of Franciscan spirituality, filling the lives of so many with an exuberance and musicality rarely witnessed before in the pursuit of holiness. Between Francis' own exemplary life and the Franciscan *élan vital* impregnating the happenings of life with so much joy, an actual theology of the earth giving the planet the sacred status she deserves has become a a real possibility today.

After suffering for a year in prison, fighting a long illness, and finally waking up to the real meaning of Christ crucified in the image of the cross at the chapel of San Damiano, Francis answered Jesus' call to rebuild a church that had become stagnant and corrupt, by becoming "another Christ." Filled with the ardor of God's love, Francis transformed medieval Europe with his devotion to the humanity of Christ, and his love and appreciation for the whole of creation.

The culmination of Francis' mirroring of Christ, occurred on Mount La Verna in 1224, when he received the wounds of the stigmata in his body. Now the reality of the beloved's care for all beings was given actuality, not only in the actions and words of Francis, but his body, in itself, revealed that sacrificial love which goes beyond appearance, projecting a kind of beauty that has more to do with God's heart.

One of the reasons Francis is so important to the modern world is that he integrated his spirituality on the levels of body, psyche, and spirit. We know today of the necessity for integrating the spiritual realm with not only daily life and actions, but in one's body and body language. There is a magnificent tempera painting of Francis by Margaritone di Arezzo. Francis has his left hand raised in the "fear not" gesture with his palm exposing the nail wound of Jesus' crucifixion in a deep, living red. His right hand clutches the sacred book of the Bible firmly, yet giving the impression of gentle calmness. Francis' eyes look directly at you, almost questioningly, and again there is that calm intensity. Di Arezzo's painting conveys that complete integration of the Christ into the very hands and eyes of Francis; even his gestures and the dignity of his poor cloak, convey the message of the beatitudes.

Saint Bonaventure, Francis' biographer, grasped Francis' character by stating that he "symbolically showed a return to that state of original innocence through universal reconciliation with each and every thing."[24] Francis symbolized the ideal lay Christian by demonstrating a return to that universal reconciliation with all life, so necessary for people who are attempting to be Christ-like at home while washing the dishes, on the highway in a traffic jam, or, by deciding to be more than civil to the bank clerk rushing the transaction. Whether leper, wolf, lamb, or even worm, Francis embodied Christ's healing love toward all beings, never wishing to dominate through creating separation, but instead seeking reconciliation. This was the state symbolized by the garden of Eden, when humans ate no flesh food, living unashamedly without guilt, because of man and woman's shared intimacy with God which joined them in the circle of non-harming and creative reverence. God had walked with humans in the garden in the cool of the day.[25] It was sin that brought humans separation, the desire to dominate human and beast bringing forth violence, war, and now, pollution. Francis joined hands with the outcast, the mean wolf of Gubbio; he recognized through his reverence the dignity of each being in Christ.

The Franciscan theology encompassing God's love, human love, and reverence for all creation, can be seen in his *Canticle to Brother Sun*. Francis did call himself, "God's Troubadour," and the *Canticle* expressed the well-roundedness of his wholistic vision. He begins by speaking of God's ultimate mystery, that transcendence which is vital to any true peak experience:

> Most high, all-powerful, all good, Lord!
>   All praise is yours, all glory, all honour
>   And all blessing.
> To you, alone, Most High, do they belong.[26]

Francis then proceeds to portray the divine immanent presence obvious in the radiance of the sun and moon, Brother Wind and Air, Sister Water and Sister Earth, "our mother, who feeds us in her sovereignty and produces various fruits with coloured flowers and herbs."[27] Francis does not stop with God's generosity in the visible realm, but proceeds into the mystery of suffering and Sister Death, stating that death will not frighten us if we have died already to the deceptions of our own false will.

Francis was himself a bright sun illumined from within, spreading God's light on the weak and the strong, the good and the not-so-good, the beautiful and those conveying that previously-mentioned other beauty. Francis was beautiful, and he proved that we may even experience joy in the purifying process by which we may enter into the light.

2

The Need for Purification

In Christianity and Islam, the purgative way is considered the most essential foundation for spiritual development. The reason purification is viewed as so vitally necessary, is because without the grounding in interior purity and ethics, all spiritual endeavor rests on a house of cards, apt to topple at the least provocation of the false ego within or by the "temptations" of the collective current social illusions. The emphasis on purification is most interesting and profound, because it means that psychological maturity and insight are just as much dimensions of spiritual growth as are religious devotion (the first commandment), and ethical considerations (the second commandment).

If one is to love God with one's whole being and strength, one must give priority to the will of God and that takes tremendous inner conversion away from past conditionings. The same holds for loving neighbor as self; if I have not learned how to respect God's immanent presence in my own body-self, how can I love my neighbor? All the great saints in Islam and Christianity have experienced the reality of the sacred alive in their own beings, and it is this experience of loving self that they are then capable of extending to neighbor.

Purification is the cleansing process by which I am able to reach God's beingness of love and see reality with completely transformed senses:

> If we would like to clean the well of the psyche of the
> polluted rubbish which constantly flows into it by the

social currents, we must first stop the flow of such polluted matter and then find a good cleaning detergent and clean the well. Then we must let the clean water flow in.[1]

Psychology is the detergent which will eventually lead us into the realm of developing a solid spirituality. Psychology opens and cleanses us; spirituality leads us into freedom. For decades, psychology and spirituality were never separated; spiritual guides were always persons who had traveled the inner road through "knowing themselves" to integration and liberation. The teachings of Jesus and Muhammad reveal a psychological understanding that is multidimensional in terms of individual salvation and practical application to daily life occurences. When Jesus recommends the extreme purification of cutting out a troublesome eye or hand, he points to it as being preferable than that the whole body be destroyed: If your "hand causes you to sin, cut it off and throw it away; it is better to lose one of your members than that your whole body go into hell."[2] How extreme this sounds. What does this have to do with psychology? Jesus, as do the Twelve-step programs, gives a teaching on how the psyche may be cleansed and renewed. The process cannot be compromised. If, for example, I am an alcoholic, I cannot even have one drink. Better to pluck out drinking completely, than allow my entire body-self to be thrown into the hell of addiction and bondage. Jesus specifically relates these teachings to mental compulsions and the easy way that one can be lost if extreme measures of self-discipline and total reliance on God are not adopted (again, a Twelve-step parallel).

Purification, then, is a deconditioning process, a path to self-knowledge and deepening love. It is a way the saints have recognized as the beginning of true spiritual discipline, and an ongoing reflective examination as one veil reveals another more subtly embedded eventually to be removed, washed, and finally, hung out to dry in the sun of God's love and newborn discernment.

A Deconditioning Process

The Sufis have for centuries identified the purgative way with deconditioning. The time of purification is a journey of removing the veils created by one's past, one's defensive barriers, wounds, rejections, fears. To even become prepared to experience the divine, the ground has to be purified—deconditioned of all that blocks the radiance and glory of God's face:

> Under nine layers of illusion, whatever the light, on
> the face of any object, in the ground itself, I see your
> face.[3]

Jelalludin Rumi, one of Islam's most magnificent poets, is here describing that ground which is deeper than any illusion no matter how initially attractive, "whatever the light," which may be deceiving us. This brief poem of Rumi's correlates with John of the Cross' famous verse on how to truly enter the pure way:

> To reach satisfaction in all
> desire its possession in nothing.
> To come to possess all
> desire the possession of nothing.
> To arrive at being all
> desire the knowledge of nothing.
> To come to the knowledge of all
> desire the knowledge of nothing.

To come to the pleasure you have not
you must go by a way in which you enjoy not.
To come to the knowledge you have not
you must go by a way in which you know not.
To come to the possession you have not
you must go by a way in which you possess not.
To come to be what you are not
you must go by a way in which you are not.[4]

The deconditioning path, the path of letting go of everything, is the path to receiving that which is so much greater than the unreal possessions of the conditioned ego. John elaborates here on how drastic the deconditioning process must be. So extreme, in fact, that in another work, John says if you *see* an "angel of light," be careful, for it is probably a disguise, deceiving you into believing you do not need the total deconditioning process. Beware of voices, inspirations, psychic powers. The Sufis also teach such wariness because the difference between the person who becomes grounded in that glorious Face, and the one who is tricked by the ego's games, is the difference between genuine holiness and grandiose charlatanism.

The primary work is to come closer to God, and to share that love with humanity and all of creation. Secondary characteristics of a psychic nature will indeed appear, but one is to either hide them, or only use them to further the work of mercy. It is an interesting criterion the Sufis came up with for holiness: that the holy one is a person who has penetrated the Source of power, and the power embodied has to do *with the Source*. If an individual has not been truly deconditioned following John of the Cross' description, all his own wants, fantasies, anxieties, will color the Source, and the light we see is not an angel's but a trickster's that is only recognized by those who have themselves been washed clean.

Purification may be more extreme for some than for others. Teresa of Avila, for example, went through years of internal cleansing consisting of doubts, illnesses, even a near-death experience. Others, like Rumi, for example, go through more external sufferings of such tremendous weight, that they break through to the infinite through the horror of the situation.

Jelalludin Rumi was a scholar and lawyer who taught Quranic law. Living in thirteenth-century Afghanistan, at thirty-seven years of age, Rumi met Shamsuddīn Tabrīzī. Shams was a wandering dervish whose name in Arabic means "the sun." Rumi left his teaching to become Shams' student because Rumi said, "What I had thought of before as God, I met today in a person."[5] Rumi's former disciples were jealous of their teacher's devotion to Shams, so according to legend they murdered the old dervish. Grief-stricken and physically stooped-over in his garden, Rumi had entered that *nada* of all he had loved and treasured. At that moment as he leaned on a pole, he began to allow gravity to play with his body, turning and turning like a top around the central pivot of the pole. The more he whirled, the more his grief was lifted, until the reality of Shams' presence crossing the boundary of life and death became an ecstatic experience. Rumi is the founder of the whirling dervishes. Not to be deceived, Rumi passed over into a mystical realization because he allowed God to work through him even in his most stricken hour.[6]

The value of purification is the freedom it gives one to experience the higher stages of the mystical life. The "bad habits" of the mind are, needless to say, difficult to change, but if one comes to that inner place of detachment, and is able to watch one's own conditioned responses without acting on them—a new person is born:

If the brain and the belly are burning clean . . .
every moment a new song comes out of the fire.

A table descends to your tents,
Jesus' table.
Expect to see it, when you fast, this table
spread with a different kind of food . . .[7]

The Goal Is Emptiness

Emptiness is the state of complete interior receptivity
to God, which only occurs when the "brain and belly are
burning clean." Notice that, for Rumi, being "pure," being
clean is not enough; one's entire motivation must be like
an intense flame hoping for Jesus' table "spread with a
different kind of food."

The fasting Christian and Islamic mystics speak of,
has to do not only with physical control of the appetites,
but much more profoundly, a burning clean of all that
would interfere with the gift of divine love and enlightenment. In Philippians we read, "have this mind among yourselves, which is yours in Christ Jesus, who though he was in
the form of God, did not count equality with God a thing
to be grasped, but *emptied himself*."[8]

If even the Christ emptied himself, the injunction
states how important it is for us to obtain this mind, this
consciousness, of pure openness. An openness to the spirit
and truth of God's guidance only occurs after the deconditioning process when the person achieves an inner clarity as to the workings of her own psyche and behavior.
Thus, she is able to stand back in detachment from her
past reactive patterns, turning instead to that space of emp-

tiness within the heart where the voice of God speaks in stillness.[9]

The stillness of resting in one's deepest center gives one the ability to hear through emptiness. A new kind of being-with-oneself is born, for it is an ontology based on oneness with God and being true to the call of sacrifice in order to obtain God-consciousness.

Often a manifestation of entering the stage of empty receptivity is the gift of tears. These tears may be literal, physical weeping, or a sobbing within, releasing one from the bonds of the past. Catherine of Genoa speaks at length on the different levels of tears, and the fact that for many, the tears are not seen nor heard, but visible in the effect of creating a new person. We know today the psychological value of weeping and the importance of a person being able to remain at a level where one does not hide his feelings. In the classical mystical stages, the type of tears experienced are an indication of what one must work on and where one is being directed. Purification brings forth intense sobbing, a weeping of brokenness and sadness at how far one is from being close to God, one's deepest self, and the community of the earth.

Tears are the continuation of purgation, even on the highest level, "for the cure comes from tears."[10] Even when we are in the highest stages of closeness to God, tears will clear the way. It is said that Ignatius of Loyola and Francis of Assisi were almost blind from ecstatic weeping. Their brothers begged them to stop, convincing them that they would be better leaders and guides with their sight intact.

> Behold, thou desirest truth in the inward being;
>   therefore teach me wisdom in my secret heart.
> Purge me with hyssop, and I shall be clean;
>   wash me, and I shall be whiter than snow.[10]

Tears sharpen that inner emptiness of constant listening to the voice of divine presence within one's own psyche and in the external world around us. The mystics have always recognized the interconnection between one's interior life and events brought into our existence to guide us and help us grow. "Whithersover ye turn, there is the Face of God."[11]

The Christian Desert

A Christian's life is determined by one signpost, and one signpost alone, namely, the life and meaning of Jesus' life. Jesus began his mission by first going to the desert for forty days and we, too, are called to such a profound experience of purification. Throughout the centuries Christian spiritual writings have emphasized the importance of "cleaning one's own house," and this has remained a constant focus for spiritual actualization. Jesus' centrality, the reality of the purity of his being in oneness with God has, and still remains, the devotee's own paradigm.

The symbol of the desert was an actual geographic reality in the days of Jesus' life on earth, and in the early Middle Eastern communities that thrived in ascetical solitude. However, in the early and Middle Ages, the desert became a symbol for that internal purification readying one to embody that new self born through grace and effortful cleansing. John of the Cross gives a powerful description of the necessity for purgation and the rewards to be gained after that dark night:

> The soul is left in a dryness and distress proportionate with its habitual natural affections (whether for divine or human things), so that every kind of demon may be

debilitated, dried up, and tried in the fire of this divine contemplation, as when Tobias placed the fish heart in the fire [Tb. 6:8], and the soul may become pure and simple, with a palate purged and healthy and ready to experience the sublime and marvelous touches of divine love. After the expulsion of all actual and habitual obstacles, it will behold itself transformed in these divine touches.[12]

The habits that today we would call conditioned patterns (John's "demons"), must be debilitated and dried up; proportionate to the attachment we have to maintaining such addictions in the face of losing touch with who we really are. The fire of the desert detaches us from our clinging, and though this can be terribly painful, this prepares us for the divine touches which are born in a pure heart. John never avoids confronting the habits that hold one back from true transformation, for he has experienced God's love, and therein knows the glory of a healthy and renewed spirit.

There have been countless saints, theologians, mystics, who have described these same stages of purgation and transformation throughout Christian history. Some have done this through the written word, some in their lives, many integrating the motivation to become one with God with a constant returning to that internal altar of sacrifice.

> O sweet cautery,
> O delightful wound!
> O gentle hand! O delicate touch
> That tastes of eternal life
> And pays every debt!
> In killing You changed death to life.[13]

The wounds of purgation sting, but their healing is sweet when touched by that eternal hand which can pay every debt of the past with newness of life born out of the death of the conditioned ego. How difficult the process can be, every mystic has attested to, and every modern psychologist will demonstrate. But the price of liberation seems small, in comparison to the freedom and love of a house built on a solid foundation.

Christian purification is also identified with the persecution and crucifixion of Jesus. We, too, who follow in the innocent One's way, will be persecuted and called to die many deaths to the false illusions of the individual and collective ego. Every Christian is asked to choose between the way of sacrifice and the quick-fix solution of a means to an end. The Christian purification process is a commitment to the means—how one behaves *on the way*—just as it is to the goal of union with God. God is near only insofar as we act within that presence which looks deception in the eye, and although aware of the possible agony ahead, courageously embodies truth.

Obeying the Call

The Prophet, Muhammad himself, went into the mountains, emptied himself, and remained still in order to hear the voice of God. Thus it was that the Qur'an was written by one who, in solitude and quiet receptivity, heard the revelations of God through his own complete submission of ego. In Islam, a Muslim is literally a "submitter to God," one who submits all that they are to God's will. Muhammad is the supreme example of obedience in the mountain desert to the power of transcendence speaking through an imma-

nent instrument. Muhammad risked everything, even believing he had lost his sanity, to place God first.

During the purgative experience, it is not unusual to
enter the shadowy realm between madness and final release in lucid sanity. Muhammad's old psyche, when transformed in the clear mountain air, was not accustomed to
the new self. It took time, and the love and support of his
wife Khadija, for Muhammad to gain confidence that what
he had actually experienced was a call to not only a new
direction in his own life, but a message for others to hear
as well. Thus it was that Muhammad, when ready, went
forth, and in his own lifetime achieved the conversion of
most of Arabia to Islam.

"I am with those whose hearts are broken for My
sake."[14] So states the Quranic traditional additions to Muhammad's revelations. If the Prophet himself had to be
broken of all that blinded him to witnessing the sacred
vision we, too, must be broken to attain purity of heart.
"We are like the lyre, that Thou pluckest."[15] However, Allah is only able to pluck our self, if that self has become
musically attuned, and at one with all that is truly merciful
and just.

Being a "submitter to God" is literal in Islam. From
how one prays in bodily posture, prostrate and receiving,
to how one internally opens the psyche through devotional
prayer to a single-minded purpose. Muslims hope to become instruments of Allah, every dimension of life filled
with numinous presence if one is able to act through God.
Rumi's famous *Creed of Love* describes the effort involved
in such purgative union:

> One went to the door of the Beloved and knocked.
> A voice asked, "Who is there?"
> One answered, "It is I."

The voice said, "There is no room for Me and Thee."
The door was shut.
After a year of solitude and deprivation, One returned
    and knocked.
A voice from within asked, "Who is there?"
One said, "It is Thee."
And the door was opened.[16]

The goal of the Sufi is to become so at one with God, that "me" is no longer even heard. This type of total commitment to God is possible through the necessary solitude and "deprivation" of addictive habits of mind and body which may be obliterated through the eventual process of purification. Whether the internal desert or the pure mountain, the seeker is aiming to achieve a unity within, which is possible for one whose eyes remain on the vision of divine revelation.

Go die, sire, before thy death,
So that thou wilt not suffer the pain of dying.
Die the kind of death which is entrance into light,
Not the death which signifies entrance into the grave.[17]

This theme of the first death being the death of the false ego is also articulated by Francis of Assisi. If this first death is truly experienced, the "second" death of physically dying is no longer terrifying, for one has encountered God beyond the life-death boundary of space and time. If one wishes to save one's life, paradoxically, one must be able to die to every attachment blocking entrance into the light. This is a universal theme, in Islam and Christianity,[18] and both strongly espouse an extreme purificatory process which would leave very little smog in the psyche to obscure that divine radiance both infinite and finite.

Jelalludin Rumi

When one reads the poetry of Rumi one is transported directly into the experience being articulated. How Rumi achieved such mastery may have to do with the fact that he had a unique gift of being able to make the experience, and the words pointing to such a reality, click in the reader's own heart. For example: "Therefore in outward form Thou art the microcosm,/ while in inward meaning Thou art the macrocosm."[19] Drawing the reader into an interior comprehension uniting the internal and external manifestations of the divine, Rumi calls us into that deep center where the sacred radiates in all aspects of reality. There is no separation between that which is obviously form, and the inner meaning creating the particular form. The goal of spiritual life here is for one to be able to perceive the One speaking through these many manifestations of reality.

> Wherever you go, you are with me still, you who are my eyes and my brightness; if you will, draw me to drunkenness, if you will, transport me to annihilation.
>
> Know that the world is like Mount Sinai, and we like Moses are seekers; every moment an epiphany arrives and cleaves the mountains asunder.[20]

The epiphany Rumi is speaking about is that total annihilation which cleaves even mountains asunder revealing the ultimate source of all being. Rumi vividly calls on traditional Judeo-Christian-Islamic themes to convey that purification of "no compromise" which leads to the divine encounter. The ego must be cracked in order for the all-One who is always present to become obvious:

Don't forget the nut, being so proud of the shell,
The body has its inward ways,

The five senses. They crack open,
And the Friend is revealed.

Crack open the Friend, you become
the All-One.[21]

Even beyond the Friend is the All-One, the essence of
life reached through a breaking process creating a wider
space within for the devotee to experience the very core of
being. It is important to reflect on the fact that, for Rumi,
although the experience leading to the cracking of the ego
may be an agonizing one, the result is sweet. In this next
stanza, again, drawing on a traditional theme, Rumi ex-
presses succinctly how our attitudinal awareness affects
our approach to the world:

Christ is the population of the world, and every object
as well. There is no room for hypocrisy. Why use bitter
soup for healing when sweet water is everywhere?[22]

"Why use bitter soup for healing when sweet water is
everywhere?" Rumi's poetic imagery helps us enter that
realm of spiritual purification that goes to the deepest levels of mystical oneness. The Christ is the population of the
world; to deny this reality, is to deny the immanence of
one's Islamic heritage, and therefore, to be a hypocrite. To
acknowledge that Christ is in everyone, and even in every
object as well, is to live one's faith without ego's interfer-
ence. Pure vision sees the sweet water everywhere, sees the
Christ in all, allows every moment to contain an epiphany.
For Rumi, the transcendent revealed in immanence is the

end of purification, and is such a powerful experience, that one is no longer even cognizant of past wounds:

> Something opens our wings. Something
> makes boredom and hurt disappear.
> Someone fills the cup in front of us:
> We taste only sacredness.[23]

Rumi begins this verse with the word "something," repeated twice. As the person deepens in purity, the object-like "something," is transformed into "Someone." Rumi here is pointing to a psychological, along with a spiritual truth. As the person breaks through the veils of illusion, one of the most important breakthroughs is consciousness of God as a "Thou." No longer an I-It relationship, the I is directly in touch with the divine Thou. For Rumi, this metamorphosis bridges the human and divine sphere. Just as human love deepens into a full acknowledgment of the other's Thouness, so in spiritual enlightenment, as purification continues, the awareness of God's "Thou" imprinting reality, becomes more and more of a continual conscious perception. I am not separate from God, but united to the sacred presence of Allah, through all pulsating reality. Rumi, for all his profound poetic expression, has a knack for ordinary imagery which may explain the immediate effectiveness he has on his listeners. Take this next verse, so simple, yet explaining perfectly volumes of theology on the difference between I-It and I-Thou relationships:

> What I most want
> is to spring out of this personality,
> then to sit apart from that leaping.
> I've lived too long where I can be reached.[24]

To contain even a speck of the ego-personality pulls us into darkness, makes us cling to that old personality frightened of leaping into the One, the Thou of endless delight.

Teresa of Avila

Teresa integrated spirituality and psychology in such a unified form that one cannot be separated from the other in her works. She knew the cartography of the inner psyche because she had experienced the journey every step of the way, and knew all the rivulets and shadowy valleys leading to self-knowledge and union with God.

Union with God was imaged by Teresa as a crystal castle. The purgative journeying into the castle brought pain and, finally, the ultimate triumph of seeing each of one's darkest demons clearly through the crystal's transparency. In her *Life,* Teresa compares the soul's crystalline divinity to a polished mirror; any area that has not been purified will blacken the mirror making one unable to *see* one's truest form. Teresa never lost sight of the goal of union with God, but she knew the value of continual purgation in order to achieve such a state of diamond-like clarity: "For never, however exalted the soul may be, is anything else more fitting than self-knowledge."[25] This is why Teresa was a "psychologist." She equated purgation with self-knowledge. Knowing one's motivational intricacies, habits, and good points, meant coming closer to God, to that ultimate perfection of love. One had to know how to remain centered through re-examining the dark shadows which would only really disappear through the healing grace and power of God.

It is difficult to encapsulate Teresa's spirituality; she is simultaneously a warm empathizer to all human flaws and sufferings, while demanding the utmost discipline and courage, so that each of us may enter that castle of freedom and bliss. She is famous for her humor, profundity, and love. On the sometimes excruciating aspects of purification:

> Once, Saint Teresa was amorously complaining to God in prayer about her sufferings and trials. She heard the Lord telling her: "Teresa, so do I treat My friends!" making her thereby understand the purificatory character of suffering. But Teresa, who knew already, answered boldly: "That's why you have so few [friends]."[26]

Part of Teresa's timeliness and appeal, for all that she lived in the sixteenth century, lies in her levelheadedness, the fact that she always kept her feet solidly on the ground. She challenges the stereotypic view of mystics as "airheads," because she always followed Jesus' example of embodied love, knowledge, and teaching.

For Teresa, mysticism with a Christic character, looks at evil unblinking, with "no better weapons than those of the cross."[27] The power of the Teresian outlook is based on her faith that God is truth; to deviate from the truthfulness of a situation is to deny the extraordinary power of the cross, because truth often demands sacrificing the illusory glitter of the individual and collective ego. Teresa speaks of the "lies, the demons" within as more dangerous than outside evil. If inner illusions and neuroses have not been properly examined and healed, it is virtually impossible to detect them in society. In fact, looking at the woundedness and confusion within, is for Teresa, the arduous task: "It seems to me that all the contempt and trials one can endure in life cannot be compared to these interior battles."[28] If the interior battles are fought, Teresa later states, "any disquiet and war can be suffered if we find peace where we live [within] . . ."[29]

So it is also an aim of the purgative journey to release a person into the freedom of truth and peace. One is no longer constricted by the bonds of psychological baggage, nor societal impositions blocking the road to sanctity. A person is freed through internal battles, prioritizing union with God and imaging the divine in one's own being. God's being becomes one's own, and the separating forces of evil are extinguished in the deepening awareness of one's true ontological identity. What now occurs in the individual is the transformation of the personality into a sacred presence. Teresa spent long years battling her demons and she rose not only to express her own liberation through God, but founded the Discalced Carmelite Order reforming the decadent practices of her time. Her purification birthed into being a radiating sanctity affecting the environment around her "because the ontological weight of a divinised person is greater than anything else."[30] Teresa conquered her own inner noise and destructiveness, and thereby gave the world, in her writings, a clear elaboration of the journey for centuries to come, and she also, through the Discalced Carmelites, continued a tradition of contemplative prayer which may still lead people of all walks of life into the crystalline center of the divinizing castle.

Because of Teresa's extreme humility, she reaches into the hearts of anyone seeking a relationship with God. Her stature appears to come from an ability to communicate the most spiritual truths in metaphoric and understandable language. She was not trying to impress with her writings but, rather, hoping to convey the need for and the steps into life's most important journey. Like Muhammad, she fought the fight privately, releasing all the inner knowledge and psychological intuition into articulate forms for others to benefit from. Like Muhammad, too, she never forgot the lowly, and though one might be in external circumstances of comfort, on the interior playing ground, we all face the same army, and the same freeing beloved.

> Hence, for love of God be very careful. There must be war in this life. In the face of so many enemies it's not possible for us to sit with our hands folded; there must always be this care about how we are proceeding interiorly and exteriorly.[31]

3

Transformation

The word "transformation" refers to a complete re-making, whether on the organic level of metamorphosis from cocoon to butterfly, or interiorly within the spiritual self. The remaking that takes place in an individual through the death of the false ego is one of resurrection: "The ego's likeness is an autumn within which a garden is concealed. When the spring-spirit arrives, the garden smiles from within."[1] Here, and in the following verse, the Muslim Rumi often compares the coming of the Spirit and the remaking taking place within the individual to spring.

> God who turns fire into trees and rosegardens
> can also make this world a place without harm.
> God who produces roses from the midst of
> thorns can make our December spring.[2]

For the Christian, Easter is surely the central message of the Christ. To be born anew after the crucifixion of the conditioned ego, is the spiritual second birth into the king-dom of truth within the center of this newly resurrected one. This internal reality is expressed as a lived awareness of Jesus' teachings.

Many Christians today are indeed focusing their spiri-tuality on the risen Christ. It is the reality and archetype of resurrection embodying a transformation of the personal-ity from victim to conqueror: "Put off your old nature . . .

and be renewed in the spirit of your minds, and put on the new nature created after the likeness of God in true righteousness and holiness."[3]

The renewal that takes place in the Christian mystic and Sufi, is one which transforms from within, eventually affecting the environment. This is an ancient philosophical idea positing the theory that being affects doing. *Who one is* will not only influence what one does, but will create an external influence in conjunction with the level of centeredness embodied in the person. This theory is also in agreement with modern physics, connecting mind to the actions and substance of matter. Saint Bonaventure stated it thusly: "The more power is unified, the more it is infinite."[4] That is, the more completely unified one is within, the more the power of the infinite is able to gain expression through us. The fourteenth-century Christian classic, *The Book of Privy Counseling,* describes such a reality in almost contemporary language:

> Be spiritually united to God without any fragmentation and scattering of your mind. God is your being and in God, you are what you are, not only because God is the cause and being of all that exists, but because God is *your* cause and the deep center of *your* being. Therefore, in this contemplative work think of your self and of God in the same way: That is, with the simple awareness that God is as God is, and that you are as you are. In this way your thought will not be fragmented or scattered, but unified in God who is all.[5]

Therefore, the transformation that takes place in the center of a purified heart, is actually a *return* to an original state of oneness with God. All that separated us from the divinity within has melted away, and we are now renewed

in our minds to express through the whole person our true
nature as imagers of the Spirit. The process sounds so
simple, but in actuality it rarely occurs at once, or even in a
lifetime. We must continually go forward in union, yet look
toward psychological issues that may still be hindering us
from actualizing our full potential. The beauty of the transformative process lies in the fact that the closer we come to
God, the easier it is to delve into the unconscious, and
uncover further blockages. The mystics speak of this growing facility as a result of entering into oneness with God.
The perspective emphasized then, is not that of the conditioned ego but, rather, of the transcendent self. Some issues may take enormous reflective work and time, yet in
other areas, because of the increasing integration within,
one passes quickly into a newfound freedom from the
ego's old fears and illusions.

I have found the soul of souls.
Let this soul of mine be taken.

I've passed beyond my very ego.
I've removed the veils before me.

I am together with the Friend.
Let these doubts of mine fall away.

My own ego abandoned me.
The Friend took everything I had.

I became tired of twoness
and ate at the table of Oneness.

I have found the honey of honeys.
Let this hive of mine be given away.[6]

A New Person

Who is this new person guided by Spirit and truth? Often the person who goes through transformation describes the new foundation in the transcendent as a state so different from the prison of the ego, it is as if she literally has become someone else.

> If you lose yourself
>   on this path
> you will know in certainty:
>   God is you, you are God.[7]

Sufism and Christianity state that the greatest obstacle in spiritual development is fear. To "lose" oneself in God is frightening when the ego has built up convenient defenses creating the illusion of control and security. When Jesus says: "Fear not, it is I,"[8] an entire spirituality is born, abandoning ordinary consciousness through the request that we join him "walking on the water" of faith and surrender. To become immersed in the divine to the extent of declaring that "God is you, you are God," is a step into mystery which only reveals its freedom *after* the step has been taken. Faith then, is that inner "yes" to all we possibly can be without unnecessary baggage of the needs of the false ego. To walk on the waters of sacred wonder and liberation, is to free oneself from the heaviness of the past. The Sufis have a story which illustrates this truth and our often pathetic desire to cling to the ersatz securities of the ego:

> "I want to learn to swim."
> "Do you want to bargain about it?"
> "No. I only have to take my ton of cabbage."
> "What cabbage?"

"The food which I will need is on the other island."
"There is better food there."
"I don't know what you mean. I cannot be sure. I must
    take my cabbage."
"You cannot swim, for one thing, with a ton of cabbage."
"Then I cannot go."[9]

And for many, the thought of abandoning the ton of cabbage which in actuality would drown them as they tried to swim, is more frightening than to swim freely in the water, and eventually find even better food on the other island. The new person, therefore, is the one who is willing to enter the waters of the unconscious, and delve into the depths of one's own personal mysteries, as well as the deepest center within, in which God is the center of all that we are.

The new person is enlivened on every level of the body, emotions, mind, and spirit, by the conscious awareness that Being penetrates all reality within and without the person. Therefore, to be unified with the ontic center within, is to be at one with God in this one's center and, further, to give forth a presence of oneness emanating into the human community, and the world of nature. It was said of Francis of Assisi that he "symbolically showed a return to the state of original innocence through universal reconciliation with each and every being."[10] When the personality is transformed, the integration cannot be contained only within the person, but bursts, as it were, into the world as an embodiment of unity and caring. Francis' holiness "had such remarkable sweetness and power that it subdued [even] ferocious beasts."[11]

This new personality grounded in the divinity, projects a healing and helping reality which, like a flower in spring, has its own beauty and scent, yet always, inevitably,

affects the environment in which it is planted. Even the
solitary saint's being will reach into the world, touching
through an invisible power, without boundaries, since it is
now united to Being itself: "The universe wears a dervish
cloak patched with heavens upon heavens."[12]

Through some mysterious process, the closer the mystic comes to expressing God consciously, the closer he
comes to reflecting the heart of matter. The universe wears
a dervish cloak, that is, the harmony of the transcendent
itself is manifested in the divinized human and cosmic
worlds, these "patches" of the divine imaged in matter.
When the personality is changed, one's humanness exhib-
its an awareness of our true human place in the natural
order, so that we are not aliens to ourselves or conquerors
of nature, but conscious beings who reverentially respect
our own being along with the beingness of the world
around us. I am not separate from God, myself, people,
animals, trees but am, rather, at-one with God present in
all reality. That is the ontology of the new person as expressed by Rumi in the following poem:

Those You Are With
What is a real connection between people? When the same
    knowledge   ·
opens a door between them. When the same inner sight exists
    in you as in another, you are drawn to be companions.
When a man feels in himself the inmost nature of a woman,
he is drawn to her sexually. When a woman
    feels the masculine self of a man within her,
she wants him physically in her.

When you feel the qualities of Gabriel in you, you fly up quickly
like a fledgling not thinking of the ground.

When you feel asinine qualities in you, no matter how you try
    to do otherwise, you will head toward the stable . . .
Always search for your innermost nature in those you are with.
As rose-oil imbibes from roses.
Even on the grave of a holy man, a holy man lays his face
and hands and takes in light.[13]

Guided by the Spirit

The secret of a spirituality of wholeness lies in the internal integration of the individual apparent in a harmony of psyche and soma. In Sufism and Christianity, the integrator is the Spirit. It is the Spirit that directs through situational guidance obvious to the one who is receptive. For example, we become receptive to the meaning of certain events which happen to appear in our lives coincidentally with specific insights gained interiorly, through dreams or the wisdom of contemplative prayer. And, in both traditions, we encounter much instruction on the Spirit's actions revealed through the patterns and processes of nature:

> For every creature is by its nature a kind of effigy and likeness of the eternal Wisdom, but especially one which in the book of Scripture has been elevated through the spirit of prophecy to prefigure spiritual things . . .[14]

This excerpt from Bonaventure, although written in the thirteenth century, contains an organic and wholistic perspective which makes his insights still pertinent today. In fact, had the European west followed Bonaventure's integrative mystical theology, rather than the Thomistic emphasis on separating spirit and matter, perhaps the present alienated quality of modern life could have been avoided. In any event, in the above quote Bonaventure gives direction on how the eternal wisdom of God is revealed through the nature and actions of our fellow creatures. The prophetic dimension prefiguring "spiritual things" has a distinctly Jungian ring, because there is no separation between the inner reality of the psyche and the natural order, what Carl Jung called *synchronicity.* Again, in the words of Bonaventure:

> From all this, one can gather that from the creation of the world the invisible attributes of God are clearly seen, being understood through the things that are made . . . and most especially, a creature which God willed to institute as a symbol and which has the character not only of a sign in the general sense but also of a sacrament.[15]

The sacramental aspect embodied in the symbol is given by and through the Spirit's presence. If we remain in the false ego, it is virtually impossible to sense the invisible divinity present sacramentally in matter. However, if we are open to the Spirit, the sacredness of immanent life becomes a continuous reality present in the most mundane and the most sublime occurences of our daily life. In the words of the Qur'an: "Truly there are signs . . . in the whole of God's creation in the heavens and in the earth."[16]

How does one come to perceive these signs sacramentally? Through an awareness which consciously chooses the Spirit's guidance over the illusory values and neurosis of the personal and socialized ego. Thomas Merton has a dramatic paragraph describing the wrestling process sifting the real from the prejudices of the false ego, as part of *The New Seeds of Contemplation:*

> Contemplation is no pain-killer. What a holocaust takes place in this steady burning to ashes of old worn-out words, clichés, slogans, rationalizations! The worst of it is that even apparently *holy* conceptions are consumed along with all the rest. It is a terrible breaking and burning of idols, a purification of the sanctuary, so that no graven thing may occupy the place that God has commanded to be left empty: the center, the existential altar which simply "is."[17]

The existential altar empty of everything but being, is an attitude able to listen to the Spirit alive speaking in the world as "is" around us. The existentiality of the altar is the fact that this centeredness is founded on living in the here and now, empty of past habits and rationalizations, even "holy" ones.

For the saints of Christ and Muhammad, holy clichés can be the most entrapping of mental constructs. Holy constructs can be used to cover serious delusions which rationalize being dutiful in the name of the laws of religion, ignoring and obstructing the spirit and heart of the tradition. So-called holy goals and holy images of oneself may be forms of addiction that lead us away from the guidance of the Spirit into the safety of preordained duties, prayers, and attitudes. The Spirit calls us into an emptiness whereby "the very heart of this work is nothing else but a naked intent toward God . . . [18]

What this signifies is that no aspect of reality is separated from the Spirit except the false ego's barriers. Francis of Assisi kissed lepers, and in our own time, we have Mother Teresa gently touching and consoling AIDS victims. Within the Islamic tradition, the great ones have also demonstrated their fearlessness of disease, death, and evil, by facing whatever God put before them, with an inner emptiness, open to revealing the Spirit, even in the most appalling circumstances. In the words of Rumi: "Every existence is poison to some and spirit-sweetness to others. / Be the Friend. Then you can eat from a poison jar / and taste only clear discrimination."[19]

Perhaps one of the genuine lessons of Spirit-guidance is love. Not the false mercy of the self-righteous fundamentalist, but the love of the saint who perceives clearly the divine shining in the multifarious forms of life. What to the norms of cultural prejudice seem ugly or "poisonous," may in fact, be the hidden pearl of spirit-sweetness. The Spirit's guidance takes us beyond shallow opinions and turns us toward a receptivity that is clear, solid, and unmasked. We enter into what Merton describes as a "deep refinement of spirit, a peacefulness, a tact and a common sense without which there is no sane morality."[20]

Guidance by the Spirit calls us into a widening and deepening of ourselves, a purification and "sanity," enabling us to release the potential within our being into an actualized wholeness. Existentially, we now live with open eyes, feet solidly planted on the ground, and our heart united to the transcendent God. The Sufis' describe the human task therein as one which "in this world, is to cleanse the heart, polish it, and ultimately to make of it a perfect mirror reflecting God."[21]

Discernment

The role of discernment in the transformative process is essential because discernment is that subtle wisdom which can ably tell if it is truly the voice of the Spirit speaking, or the ego-trickster persuading us to take a path of ego-blockage. In the Christian Middle Ages, a spiritual director was entitled a "Reader of Hearts," for this one could look behind the mask of the person right into the heart's motives. The ability to read hearts became evident only after years of self-analysis, prayer, and most probably, the scrutiny of another older, and more experienced, spiritual director. The total honesty and touching love demanded of a spiritual director usually would take years to develop. It is an ability described in many Sufi stories of Masters who see through the obvious to the core reality, bringing this reality to the forefront either through an action, a word, or a story. For example, in the following anecdote about Sufi Master Rabi'a:

"What miracles have you done, if any, Rabi'a?"

"If I were to admit to a miracle

I'd be worried it might bring in money—

So my answer is: not one!"[22]

We know that the hagiographic legends surrounding Rabi'a contain one miracle account after another. Yet, Rabi'a herself knows well the detrimental role they can play in pushing someone from focusing on inner work. If one concentrates on psychic powers, it is often an evasion, a running away from the necessary efforts of purifying the ego, and falling into the much less demanding glitter of immediate distractions. Rabi'a, therefore, disavows any miracle-working power on her part, in favor of seeming as ordinary as anyone, and therein helping each person on whatever her spiritual level, to be aware of God's presence and the inner work involved in integration and holiness. Rabi'a's discernment places a value on the inner life over outward show. Her judgments, then, will be colored by actions demonstrating a wisdom based on ultimately being-at-one with God and self first.

The foundation of discernment is the value system of the one reaching for balanced wisdom. Therefore, the combination of values and common sense, love and honesty, should be uncompromising in the individual's life, along with the spiritual guidance given to others. "The aim of our charge is love that issues from a pure heart and a good conscience and sincere faith."[23] Nothing sensationalist is quoted here from the New Testament, but simple virtuous qualities which will give one a solidity of faith and the expansive ability to discern the subtlest of situations. The more grounded the person is in purity, good conscience, and sincere faith, the greater his facility with people and events which to someone less centered could be ethically confusing. That is why the Christian saint or Sufic saint will dwell more on his own ordinariness and the rock-like qualities of love and truth in discerning, rather than strange interpretations, psychic phenomena, or spectacular "wowing" experiences.

Jesus makes the remarkable statement that: "Every one who is of the truth hears my voice."[24] Accordingly, discernment may be described as an increasing ability to detect the truth in oneself, as well as, in the reality-base of other people's motives and actions. To uncover the truth, is a deepening ability to uncover the clues within inner and outer circumstances that are revealing the Spirit's guidance.

Why is the truth sometimes difficult to find? Again, the response offered by both Islamic and Christian teachers, is that the personal and collective ego protects itself by any means, and one of the easiest is to lie to oneself, or, through a collective social denial, about what is *really* occurring situationally. An example in Islam, is the story of the Sufi martyr al-Hallāj (d. 922 C.E.), who was murdered for stating that he was one with God. The truth surfaces in this real-life drama, even after al-Hallāj's martyrdom: Each of his body pieces which had been hacked and thrown into the Tigris river, surfaces singing, "Anā' l-Hagg" / "I am the Truth."[25] After going through such a grim death, the oneness between al-Hallāj and the divine One, is still witnessed through song soaring beyond death.

We see the importance of embodying the truth no matter the cost, also exemplified in Jesus standing before Pilate. Pilate declares, "What is truth?" since he is blind to the incarnation of truth standing before his eyes.[26] And Jesus, perceiving Pilate's blindness, says no more; his silence speaks as loudly of truth as his words.

If we visually place ourselves at the scenes of al-Hallāj's martyrdom, and Jesus' interrogation by Pilate, it is incredible, that what is actualized, through being and action, is Truth itself.

Rumi helps us, with an interesting metaphor, on how we can individually begin to cultivate an inner awareness of truth. It is evidently a simultaneously simple and profound listening to one's motives through the body, as described in the following poem:

On Resurrection Day

> On Resurrection Day your body testifies against you.
> Your hand says, "I stole money."
> Your lips, "I said meanness."
> Your feet, "I went where I shouldn't."
> Your genitals, "Me too."

They will make your praying sound hypocritical.
Let the body's doings speak openly now,
without your saying a word,
as a student's walking behind a teacher
says, "This one knows more clearly
than I the way."[27]

The opposite of discernment is to follow a mental addiction enacted through the body, whether it be stealing, meanness, an inappropriate path or sexual behavior. Rumi is the poet of love, and usually extols sexuality with a frankness and balanced attitude, rare in the annals of religious writers. Be that as it may, in the almost comical line quoted above, Rumi is speaking of a type of sexual behavior, motivated by an individual's lack of interior insight, and therefore, unhealthy and unhealed ego.

To listen to what we *do,* reflects back on *who we are.* Rumi recognized that the body, as such, is a great teacher of the mind's motives whether conscious or reactive. His insight into discernment is profound in terms of its implications for our physical well-being, psychic balance, and a continual ability to hear the voice of the Spirit's truth within ourselves and in the world around us.

Freedom and Limits

The freedom activated by the Spirit through transformative mysticism makes one acutely aware of limitations. The freer one becomes, the greater the awareness of the strictures on what nourishes the body-mind, what we can do to help others, and how to practically orient our lives in terms of time and effort. Hence, these limits are not imprisonments, but in a sense, freedom-givers, because we realize all the possibilities that are now open to us. We learn to choose, to discern, as a necessary dimension of liberation.

In Islam and Christianity, the foundational ethical training, in combination with self-disciplining the mind, and praying through ecstasy or desert, grounds the personality. When transformation takes place then, one does not react confusedly, because one is solidly focused on the precepts of the first two commandments which will truly bring inner peace and freedom.

The first commandment of loving God with one's whole being, heart, and strength, now is chosen freely from experienced love in the totality of union. Consequently, one goes to prayer with the hope and expectation of a continued and deepening union with God. In the words of Yunnus Emre's poem:

> You fall in love with Truth and begin to cry,
> You become holy light both inside and out,
> singing Allah, Allah.
>
> Whatever you desire, ask it of Truth.
> Be a guide on the straight path.
> The nightingale has fallen in love with the rose,
> singing Allah.[28]

When one falls in love with truth, the light shines both inside and out, because we have been awakened to the existence of the sacred alive in the interior and exterior worlds. Our entire being becomes song. Whatever we ask of truth will be granted, because our realization of truth makes us one with truth. We are not separate from God and, therefore, our intentions are aligned with the love and truth of the divine presence.

Again, due to the very fact of being united to truth, the asking will be in conjunction with the values of mercy and justice whether for oneself or others. I am free to ask for what I desire, because even my desires are centered on transcendent goals.

Emre's classic use of the symbolism of the nightingale and the rose, brings into play the Sufi metaphors for one's inner relationship with God: The nightingale is a metaphor for the soul, the rose is the manifestation of divine beauty. The use of the metaphor of falling in love, indicates that the experience of God is what is desired above all else. Hence, the song of the nightingale is the ecstatic expression of one who has found the numinous, and in the presence of such glory, bursts forth into poignant singing.

In conclusion, we may define one dimension of freedom, according to Islamic and Christian writers, as an aspect of character development which is not limited by mental attachments that may remain as neuroses. These neuroses, as noted, may turn outward into unintended forms of greed, sexual dependencies, clinging behaviors, and the rest.

Accordingly, freedom is spiritually expressed as character development. That is, wholeness of body and mind. Perhaps the true test of spiritual transformation is to see for ourselves, as Rumi previously defined, how free we really are in the actions of the body, and the repeated conditioned patterns of the mind. The foundation of freedom, then, would be character unfoldment. If one is working from a singleminded desire to know the truth, because one *loves* truth; this leads one into the healing and bliss of inner peace, and the ultimate freedom of union with God.

The Divine Child

The tremendous undertaking and victory of overcoming conditioned mental patterns which had led to unhealthy, unfulfilling, and demoralizing habits of behavior, is described, as we noted, by Christianity and Islam, in terms of spiritual purification. The result of healing purification is the birth of the divine child within the freed person.

In the book of *Isaiah* we read: "The lion shall dwell with the lamb . . . and a child shall lead them."[29] Since both Christianity and Islam are derived from the Hebrew scriptures, the truths expounded in these earliest of scriptures is continually referred to by both of these two later traditions.

In Jungian psychology, the lion is a symbol of our most aggressive side, the lamb our passive dimension. When the two opposites are joined within, actually dwelling one with the other, a divine child is born within the center of one's being. The child then leads us into right action in accord with divine guidance, through the wonder and receptivity which children embody. It is important to note here that the divine child within is not "childish" in the worst sense of being immature or selfish, but is, rather, a qualitative character of the fully realized human being manifested in qualities such as wonder, creativity, spontaneity, love, and intuition.

In our present technologized culture, the divine child is especially relevant because, for so many people, the child-like qualities of the divine have been wounded or squelched during childhood. As adults, then, we must be healed and learn to utilize parts of the personality vital to happiness and love: love of oneself, especially in the form of bodily self-respect and behavioral self-esteem.

When Jesus stated that we must become as a child to enter the kingdom, he was speaking of this new birth and transformation through the Spirit whereby the individual is indeed changed.[30] Changed to such a degree that the transformation will actually determine whether one may enter the kingdom or not. The kingdom meaning that unity of being and consciousness, within which the person is at *home* in the oneness of the transcendent (heavenly), and the immanently (earthly), divine. We can no more enter this oned consciousness without being changed from within, than can a grasshopper become a giraffe! On the spiritual level, it is a "species-like" transformation.

According to Meister Eckhart, the sixteenth-century Dominican, the birth of God in the soul is a "breaking-through" into the "unknown territory where God dwells."[31] The change is so drastic, for Eckhart, that it is a metamorphosis into the divine as God is born within. We are made whole and holy through this change and new birth ontologically: "So a person must be penetrated with the divine presence, and be shaped through and through with the shape of God. . ."[32]

All the dimensions of the self that had perhaps been denied in childhood: the glorious pleasures of life, the quiet wisdom of the mystic, the inspiration of the natural order, become not just important to know, but theophanic experiences. When the living God is experienced as present here and now, the change to aliveness from deadened adulthood is obvious. The birth of the divine child parented by the master-self, grounded in appropriate love, knowledge, and wonder, is the actualization of resurrection within. The following poem by master Rumi, graphically describes the state of transformation, and being guided by the Spirit into everyday resurrection.

A Master of Life

> Wake up with the morning breeze
> and ask for a change. Open and fill yourself
> with the wine that is your life . . .
> Give me your excitement, but let it ground me,
> so I don't wander. Watch the ripples
> on the surface. Then launch me
> like a ship. Once I was only a piece of wood.
> Then Moses threw me down,
> and now I'm a powerful dragon. I was dead.
> Jesus raised me. Muhammad spoke,
> and this tree shimmered.
>
> Say the word again, Shams,
> so we can feel you, your light
> within everything.[33]

For Rumi, Shams, whose name in Arabic literally means, "the sun," is the embodiment of mastering life. Shams was an old nomadic dervish who was Rumi's mentor. The divine light which is so clear in Shams' presence, is also the numinous present "within everything." The significance of Shams' mastery of life to Rumi, cannot be overestimated. For Rumi, Shams' person is the way, the door, to how one should model one's own life. Shams is the paradigmatic Sufi.

In the beginning of the poem, we see that Rumi is speaking of his own personal life. He begins rightly with waking, the first action of the day. He tells us to ask for a change, that is, the continued growth in experiencing the rich "wine" of our life through receptivity to the Spirit. Rumi then instructs God (!), to give him the excitement of metamorphosis, but not to neglect *grounding* him. This is typical of a true master of life in the Spirit, as we have noted before; that no matter what the ecstasy, the excitement, there always exists the necessity to remain grounded. It is the person who gets carried away by blinding excitement who will lose the divine center of the quiet voice within.

In any event, Rumi, then, turns symbolically to the traditional figures of Judaism, Christianity, and Islam, to articulate how he was completely remade. Rumi's images are not only archetypal, but riveting in the original usage he assigns to them: To proceed from a plain piece of wood implying lifelessness and boredom, to a powerful dragon through Moses' intervention is the first image. In the next image, Rumi describes himself as really dead, until Jesus raises him up through transformation. And, finally, Rumi hints at the tree shimmering, a symbol of the realized self. With these three quintessential images, Rumi, through the main figures of each tradition, points to the transformation process that is such an essential aspect of their teachings.

In summary, there is a verse in the Qur'an which speaks of the "eye of realized discernment."[34] Therefore, the goal of transformation is an awareness that is able to discern distinctions between negative forces within and without oneself, and true guidance of the Spirit established through love and truth. The transformative goal is an awakened consciousness attuned to what is occurring within one's own psyche on the road to healing and union with God. When one is awakened, even in the social circumstances of the world, one is able to discern, and be an example of, mercy-filled truth.

Christianity and Islam speak of realized discernment as a gift; earned indeed through self-effort, but given freely as one continues on the path of unifying love: For God has "given thee abundance."[35]

4

Union

The master of life in the Spirit, tries to live as close to God as possible. There are, of course, the inevitable failures, especially when the old mental patterns interfere with what is being established through discernment within one's newfound outlook and life. However, if one keeps her inner eye focused on the divine within, the union with the Spirit will gradually dominate the personality. Joy and freedom, perhaps only experienced in very early childhood, will come to be a daily occurrence in one's everyday existence.

For both Christianity and Islam, the state of union with God is our true existential state. We were created to live life joined to the sacred, and to manifest the reality of God's presence through our own being. Both traditions hold to union as the goal of spiritual development, and the path which will lead to human fulfillment. In the words of Shāh Ne'matollāh:

> I beheld my essence. What I saw
> Was like the very light of the eye itself:
> How wonderful that a single Essence should
> Refract itself like light, a single source
> Into a million essences and hues.[1]

To behold one's essence leads to an embodiment of that essence in our own individuated way. The point is, that when one perceives his real identity, as Being's own essence, that is, as God-likeness, petty cares and frustrations fall away, and one is led to truly be the "light of the eye itself."

One's own daily words, actions, involvements, will then be colored by the million hues which actually are a refraction of the single source, namely, God's essence. Consequently, there is no separation between our own union with God, the single essence, and the millions of essences and hues, that the essence emanates through the material order.

In the dramatic narrative on *The Death of al-Hallaj*, Satan is described as "a mad ascetic, / Who couldn't bear beauty being fleshy, / Visible tangible sensible real."[2] In other words, evil tries to make of reality something it intrinsically is not. That the transcendent is made "visible tangible sensible real," through life on earth in people, and the creation, would mean that one would plunge into the visible, through commitment and love, as part of one's union with God.

Evil, on the other hand, distorts what is real, by trying to make of what is into a controlled version of its own distorted needs. One would, then, either broaden evil into a collective misshape of the sacred, and/or, narrow the distortion to suit a personal neurosis. In any of these scenarios, evil becomes a cumulative shadow of fear, covering reality with all sorts of crazed interpretations, which block the simple beauty of God present in the here and now. Accordingly, union with God leads to the opposite realization from that of "Satan's"; it is, rather, a growing appreciation of the miraculous quality of the divine become flesh and earth, star and thought.

Jesus' healing miracles, for example, point to the reality that God has created us for full, "earthly," lives:

> And a leper came to him beseeching him, and kneeling said to him, "If you will, you can make me clean."

Moved with pity, he stretched out his hand and touched him, and said to him, "I will; be clean." And immediately the leprosy left him, and he was made clean.[3]

Jesus' healing miracles epitomize the reality of the divine working through the natural order. What else would be the significance of God made flesh, if not to heal the sufferings of the flesh? Jesus always took care of the basic needs of people before preaching to them: he either fed them with the loaves and fishes, or cured the body's illnesses. The later development in Christianity of certain bizarre mystical sects, who developed a Manichaeistic split between spirit and matter, creating a cult of masochistic suffering, had nothing to do with the gentle founder of Christianity, who cured the sick, and soothed the distressed.

Thus, union with God implies a desire to follow the divine will, and spiritually, in order to be aligned to the divine, one's theology must be properly balanced in terms of who we are essentially, and how that essence relates to being whole in body, mind, emotions, through the Spirit's guidance. Muhammad himself, as with Jesus, did not deny the blessings of creation. For Muhammad, marriage, a love for people of every segment of society, prosperity, the sensual joys of eating and appreciating nature, were all a part of Muhammad's example and teachings. Therein, union with God has implications in the immanent order, which reflect the depth of the bond internally being strengthened with the transcendent. In the words of the Muslim poet Emre: "Wherever I looked, it was God I saw!"[4]

Since Islam and Christianity were born from the book of Genesis, the basic philosophy that creation is good, and that we humans are imagers of the divine, comes as no surprise. It is simply an important spiritual realization to continually take note of our true place, in terms of union with God, and how we reflect such a union within our own imaging of the divine. We are able to see in prayer whether we really are divine imagers in own body-self, personal relationships, work, attitude toward the planet, and commitment to collective social issues. This is a deep visualizing meditational technique, whereby the practitioner weighs his own knowledge of his true potentialities, and how well those potentialities are being actualized within his own being and life. Modern self-help programs are filled with just such insights, and in many ways they are the same ones presented in the religious traditions; that is, the closer one comes to imaging God, the closer one comes to existentially living one's potentialities.

How one becomes free of the "demons" within one's own mind, one's own neuroses, and negative behavioral patterns, is by replacing such limited images of oneself with more divinized images in keeping with who one can be through transformation. The saints of Islam and Christianity did not shut themselves off from metamorphosis and life, but brought contemplation into the arena of life as a dynamic transformative power grounded in what union with God can do *as a transformative power.*

At One with God

In the Christian *Cloud of Unknowing,* we read: "For the work of perfect love which begins here on earth is the same as that love which is eternal life; they are but one."[5] I would like to emphasize a spiritual perspective not only describing union with God within the individual's being, but how that oneness becomes an awareness of God's presence all around us. This kind of perspective, as we know, is

necessary today, for twentieth-century people are knowl-
edgeable in areas of physiology, psychology, anthropology,
sociology, ecology, and cosmology. How the human, then,
relates not only to herself, but to the universe around her,
will be assessed according to standards of wholeness now
almost universally accepted.

For example, if someone cannot deal with her past,
but denies the pain through frantic activity, we rightly discern that something is essentially wrong with this person
because of the repression of her past. Therefore, we will
bring to the perspective on healing, along with the knowledge and insights of, for example, psychological and sociological truths, the power of mystical awareness, so that she
may view herself as part of the "big picture."

Herein, she will observe how the Spirit's presence is
active in the large and the small, in her own life, and in the
forces of planets. These transcending awarenesses, what
Maslow called "peak experiences," often occur with awarenesses that view the human being in her true context as
part of a larger whole; for example classical religious experiences of God in Islam and Christianity, and experiencing
the presence of the sacred in music, the ocean, whatever
releases one from the conditioning of the ego.

Being at-one with God, indicates a centeredness that
touches all areas of life, but is usually greatly enhanced by
contemplative prayer. "For as I have said before, there
never has been and there never will be a creature so pure
or so deeply immersed in the loving contemplation of
God who does not approach God in this life through that
lofty and marvelous *cloud of unknowing.*"[6] *The Cloud of Unknowing* is a wonderful metaphor for the contemplative
experience of mystery. Within this cloud, there are no
more definitive rational explanations but, rather, an expe-

rience of God as the One beyond names and forms, in the
glory of unknowing which cannot be categorized. It is a
transpersonal experience, which St. John of the Cross describes thusly:

> And this supreme knowledge
> Is so exalted
> That no power of man or learning
> Can grasp it;
> He who masters himself
> Will, with knowledge in unknowing,
> Always be transcending.[7]

John of the Cross speaks here of a "knowledge in
unknowing." This is a paradoxical phrase, and yet, one
that is continuously expounded by Christian and Islamic
mystics. The "knowledge in unknowing," is the most "supreme knowledge," gained by the person who has mas-
tered herself.

Here we come to a key insight: that this is the knowledge of someone who is so integrally at one with her own
self and with God, that now she enters into a knowledge
experienced *in the moment*, which spontaneously helps her
to "always be transcending."

What does St. John mean by always transcending?
Transcending away from something, or transcending toward something? I believe that he is speaking of both simultaneously. That is, that one is going further and further
beyond the limits of the ego, while entering into God's
essence which cannot be defined or rationally explained.
John does explain that such a mysticism is based on union,
and the secret of transcending is the soul united to God
through love. In another verse, John elaborates on this
unity between lover and beloved:

O guiding night!
O night more lovely than the dawn!
O night that has united
The Lover with his beloved,
Transforming the beloved in her Lover.[8]

Images of lover and beloved do capture the experience of oneness, as the two become one, in and through
love. Christian mysticism has endless examples of the love
mysticism exemplified by the mystical marriage. John of
the Cross is one of the more profound theologically, but
there exist many others, who also acknowledge that they
cannot even begin to explain this experience that surpasses
the intellect, yet draws one deeper into the love of God.

Turning to the Sufis, we see the same emphasis on the
mystical marriage and, too, the countless Sufis who have
had to turn to metaphor to describe that which goes beyond rationally oriented language—for example, the following verses of Rumi, intermixing the most profound
awareness of oneness with God, with a comic image of a
man's mustache, by way of contrasting just how absurd we
humans can be in our attempt to not be our fullest selves in
union with the divine self.

Rescue this man from his mustache,
curling so proudly, while inside he tears
his hair. Married to God, married
to God, but pretending not!

Dive into the Ocean.
You're caught in your own pretentious beard
like something you didn't eat.
You're not garbage! Pearls want to be
like you. You should be with them
where waves and fish and pearls and seaweed and wind

are all one. No linking, no hierarchy,
no distinctions, no perplexed wondering, no speech.
Beyond describing.[9]

Here Rumi is tying together self-esteem and oneness
with God, being "married to God." To dive into the ocean
is to enter the mystery beyond distinctions and speech. We
are not garbage! What a line! How could one put it more
succinctly? We are being called by the "pearls," who want
to be like us! That is how intrinsically beautiful and luminous we really are; that it is the pearls who want to emulate
us. If only we would recognize who we really are, "married
to God," in that interior realm of centered oneness which is
"beyond describing."

Immortal Life

An essential element of our identity in the divine,
which surpasses even our body-mind self, is our identity as
part of the eternalness of God. We come to recognize that
we are much more than this body, than this mind. Although we come to reverence the body-mind through the
exprience of union, and our immanent identity as imagers
of God *in the world,* we also realize that we are intimately
unified with the Spirit.

In the experience of union with the Spirit, we are no
longer afraid of death, and our identity includes that of
becoming one with the invisible realm. In the words of
Hafiz of Shiraz: "The Provider revealed the secret of this
world and the next,"[10] so that I no longer contain a separation between this-worldly spirituality, and my deepest
human need to understand the meaning of life and
death.

Admittedly, people today are tired of the old religious platitudes, which emphasized relinquishing the delights of this world in favor of the afterlife. There is no escaping the fact that an unhealthy emphasis has been placed on the afterlife by both Islam and Christianity, at different times historically. However, just because such a distorted view has warped the beauty of earthly and heavenly mysticism,[11] does not mean that, in reaction, we should ignore the balance between the two, which is our true religious heritage.

The heavenly perspective helps us deal with questions of ultimate meaning. What this signifies is that when those inevitable times occur in our own lives of suffering and death, crisis, failure, and the confrontation with evil, we are able to see beyond the situation, to a meaning which may surpass the limits of earthly life.

If we take the simple example of getting old, we see that there must come a time when we have to face the oncoming of our own death, and what significance death has for us in terms of our "marriage to God." John Ruusbroec in his *Spiritual Espousals,* describes the experience of union, as dwelling in God eternally. It is an experiential continuum of existing in that center where life and death coexist together in that *mysterium tremendum* we call God. Once we reach that inner consciousness, it is as if we have touched the core of blessing itself, the "bare" nature, empty of ego-projections, and are now grounded in God alone. In the words of Ruusbroec:

> For this reason the Spirit, in the most intimate and highest part of its being, in its bare nature, ceaselessly receives the imprint of its eternal image and of the divine resplendence and becomes an eternal dwelling place of God.[12]

For Ruusbroec, death does not sting, because *in this life,* he has touched the eternal. In the highest experience of union, the intimacy with God takes the person into a realm of divine resplendence where the "imprint" of God's eternal image is stamped so dramatically upon one's experience that this joining will carry over into all areas of life, enabling one to endure the dark side of existence.

The wise one, Rabi'a, from an Islamic point of view, utilizing the Sufi image of God as friend, presents an interesting twist on how a human being might interpret death itself:

> "I am the murderer of joy," said the Angel of Death,
>
> "The widower of wives, the orphaner of children—"
>
> "Why always run yourself down?" said Rabi'a—
>
> "Why not say instead: 'I am the one who brings friend
>   and Friend together?' "[13]

We can see that, for Rabi'a, death has a more positive value in terms of bringing "friend and Friend together." With her usual sense of humor, Rabi'a swiftly changes the negative association we would naturally have with death, from the vantage point of terrible loss, to one of happiness and joining. In fact, in her parables, like so many other saints, Rabi'a actually looks forward to death. She looks forward to the ultimate joining with God, but nonetheless regards the most difficult dimension of the death-experience as the hardship of leaving those one loves in the material universe.

Love is that which links us to our loved ones and the community. To be genuinely embodied in love, then, is very different than projecting the ego onto life. The ego is another kind of death, blocking not only the experience of God connecting us to the sacred in the heavenly and the earthly, but also does not allow us to penetrate to the depth of love through relationship.

Death is feared by the ego, according to both Muslim and Christian mystics. The reason death is feared by the ego, is because death is the final annihilation of all that has blocked one from union with the divine self. The ego in its pathetic grasp for power, cannot deal with that final experience of oneness. Perhaps it is worth repeating, that the ego's grasp for power is generated by a desperate need caused by a wound to the personality. This need is an attempt to never be hurt again. The ego, therefore, except in its role as helper with basic survival needs, can become a maleficent force in one's life, to protect one from any hurtful repetitions of the original wound. Since these forces are usually created early in life, they are likely to be irrational, and more often than one would like to believe, may rule a person's entire life-cycle, from the basis of fear and the worst possible false needs.

Rumi explains what death does to the ego, and how death clears the way for freedom from fear, birthing the beauty of divinization:

> Once you have been delivered from this cage, your home will be the rosegarden. Once you have broken the shell, dying will be like the pearl.[14]

Ultimately, in Rumi's understanding, we are delivered from the cage and shell of the ego by death. We are, then, born into our true home which is like a rosegarden. Dying thus reveals the pearl, since the shell has been broken, and now we discover what has been inside protected by the soft flesh of life.

5

A God-Centered Ecology

The Garden of Life

All forms of life, including the planets, galaxies, and cosmos, were created by God as blessing revealing the image of the maker. The mythological bases of both Islam and Christianity, are founded on the Hebrew scriptures' interpretation of creation. That is, that the goodness of God is given freely, and imaged in all creatures great and small.

Sometimes the demands of survival keep us from the experience of recognizing the aspect of blessing in all life. Everyday instances, such as the miraculousness of how a baby human, or a baby fawn, are formed and brought into existence, are "common" miracles. Blessing, then, would also have to do with an attitude of gratitude, whereby we awaken to the sacred always present in the myriad events of existence.

In the book of Genesis, the creation is simply gift, a garden made with care, and in its essence, very good.[1] Our original place was to walk with God in the garden of life. The saints of Christianity and Islam, once they have entered union, long to return to the garden. In the words of John of the Cross:

> My Beloved is the mountains,
> And lovely wooded valleys,
> Strange islands,
> And resounding rivers,
> The whistling of love-stirring breezes.

The tranquil night
At the time of the rising dawn,
Silent music,
Sounding solitude,
The supper that refreshes, and deepens love.[2]

The image John used of a "supper that refreshes,"
and "deepens love," is significant. Because God rests on
the seventh day we, too, may only appreciate the garden of
life through the quiet rest obtained in that contemplative
sabbath within. Without hearing "silent music" through
"sounding solitude," we frequently cannot appreciate the
world around us. The Muslim, Shabistarī, in The *Secret
Rose Garden* writes:

Each creature has its being
From the One Name,
From which it comes forth,
And to which it returns,
With praises unending.[3]

Praise is considered by both traditions as one of the
highest forms of prayer. Praise is the gate into the garden. When the gate is opened, we see the creation in all
its magnificence. If we are too busy to enter contemplative rest, and to be reborn into praise, we lose contact
with the very heart of being alive. In the Qur'an we
read:

The seven skies, the earth, and all
that lies within them,
sing hallelujas to God.
There is nothing that does not chant God's praises,
but you do not understand their hymns of praise.[4]

In the verses that follow the above quotation from the Qur'an, we see that the reason one cannot recognize the "hymns of praise," is lack of faith.

Tawhid is Arabic for faith in the unity of all life. A God-centered ecology begins with a relationship to, and faith in, God. Without this center in one's life, according to both Sufi and Christian saints, one would lose touch (literally as well), with the source and essence of all Being. We see symptoms of this today, in people who have the greatest concern for environmental issues, but become fatigued emotionally and spiritually when they are not strengthened through a stable interior center.

Therefore, our role from a spiritual perspective, is to remain centered in the divine within, so that we may act for the good of, and appreciate the divine without.

Nonetheless, a practice to remember here, is that nature herself, whether ocean, mountain, or forest trail, can be a way of returning to center. Experiencing the sacred in the rhythms and forms of pulsating life is certainly a prayerful practice that may bring us back to a realization of numinous presence as attested to in the following verses from Job:

> But ask the beasts, and they will
>   teach you;
> the birds of the air, and they will
>   tell you;
> or the plants of the earth, and they
>   will teach you;
> and the fish of the sea will
>   declare to you.
>
> Who among all these does not know
>   that the hand of the Lord has
>   done this?

> In God's hand is the life of every
>   living thing and the breath of all
>   humankind.[5]

One of the primary religious experiences is a feeling of awe. When one enters into the natural world, the "hand of God" is obvious, so that one finds it often a spontaneous happening of having returned to center without any effort on our part. That all of creation has much to teach us has been acknowledged by the saints time and time again. It is an attitude that makes us truly stewards *with* all species, rather than exploiters who treat our earthly neighbors as objects. Our true familial relationship with all species and life is then grounded in our own earthliness: "For thou didst form my inward parts / intricately wrought in the depths of the earth."[6]

The Human Steward

Being a steward both of one's inner life and the planet, implies a guarding and valuing, a trust. In the Hebrew scriptures humans are entrusted with the fruits of the earth. This implies a *participation* in the fertility and goodness of the earth, even to the point of vegetarianism before the Fall. In Genesis 1:29, we are told, "And God said, 'Behold, I have given you every plant yielding seed which is upon the face of all the earth, and every tree with seed in its fruit; you shall have them for food.' "
Only after human beings lost their deep relationship with the divine, did they bring violence into the garden, as stated in Genesis 9:2:

> The fear of you and the dread of you shall be upon
> every beast of the earth, and upon every bird of the air,
> upon everything that creeps on the ground and all fish
> of the sea: into your hand they are delivered."[7]

The above quotations from Genesis give us the original story, and its view of why human beings changed from participators to users. The later scriptures of the New Testament and the Qur'an, along with the examples from Muslim and Christian saints, define how the human can return to the garden.

If our true role is as stewards, the question for today is, how is such a role described by these two traditions? And, further, how does this spirituality guide us into a more ecologically reasonable point of view?

I would like to spend a bit more time on the Hebrew scriptures, since they are the foundational home of Islam and Christianity, and the *weltanschauung* from which Muhammad and Jesus were nourished.

For example, one of the great wisdom figures referred to by both traditions, was Solomon. Solomon was and is an archetypal human who represented wise leadership and understanding. It is significant to note that Solomon is defined, not by his "ability to render justice—not even his ability to rule effectively . . . rather, it is his encyclopedic knowledge of his environment"[8] which describes his identity. In 1 Kings 29–33, we read:

> And God gave Solomon wisdom and understanding
> beyond measure, and largeness of mind like the sand
> on the seashore, so that Solomon's wisdom surpassed
> the wisdom of all the people of the east, and all the
> wisdom of Egypt. For he was wiser than all other
> men . . . and his fame was in all the nations round

about. He also uttered three thousand proverbs; and his songs were a thousand and five. He spoke of trees, from the cedar of Lebanon to the hyssop that grows out of the wall; he spoke also of beasts, and of birds, and of reptiles, and of fish.

Solomon then, knew his world. He was able to study, learn, and *be* in his world as a role model because of the very fact that his wisdom was based on an understanding of how trees, humans, plants, beasts, and birds all interact.

The horrible indictment of Genesis 9:2, describing the human as an enemy of the environment, may be changed. This change, though, may only come about if humanity pursues the path of stewardship and peacemaking. In the oft-quoted words of Hosea:

> And I will make for you a covenant on that day with the beasts of the field, the birds of the air, and the creeping things on the ground; and I will abolish the bow, the sword, and war from the land; and I will make you lie down in safety.[9]

Stewardship is the paradigm of human existence lived in safety and peace. It implies entrustment and caring, but more than these, stewardship goes to the heart of Jesus' and Muhammad's teachings: that we were created to come home to God.

Our home with God was symbolized by walking with the divine presence in the garden in the cool of the day. That relationship forges within us an increasing desire to be kind to all life, which in itself also reflects that divine presence. When we have learned to love our own divine nature, we will then recognize our partnership in the splendor surrounding us. And, only then, will human beings begin to be a part of the kingdom of peace on earth as described in the gospel of Mark:

> With what can we compare the kingdom of God, or what parable shall we use for it? It is like a grain of mustard seed, which, when sown upon the ground, is the smallest of all the seeds on earth; yet when it is sown it grows up and becomes the greatest of all shrubs, and puts forth large branches, so that the birds of the air can make nests in its shade.[10]

Enjoying Nature

To use nature solely for economic profit, according to Muhammad and Jesus, is to miss the point. Nature herself is a dimension of the gift of God's love to us, and defines our own humanness. To make of nature an "It" to be used, is to distort the graciousness and beauty contained in the meaning of existence. Hence, nature is to be enjoyed, cherished, reverenced.

Seyyed Hossein Nasr, one of the foremost modern scholars on Islamic spirituality, tell us that: "If virgin nature serves as support for recollection or remembrance of God, it is because it was created by the Divine Artisan, one of God's Names being *al-Ṣāni'*, literally the Divine Artisan or Maker."[11]

Accordingly, one of the contributions the religious traditions can make to the increasing technologizing of the planet is an ethic of enjoyment, and reverence for its *own sake*. The west's puritanical work ethic, and its definition of wealth as the accumulation of material goods, has defeated the entire purpose of human relatedness to the universe. If "every creature of the world is for us book, picture, and mirror,"[12] our role is, rather, to take joy in, and delight in caring and keeping a world in which we can learn and grow in wisdom.

There is indeed, irony in the fact that we have to learn all over again how to enjoy those things that children seem to have such a spontaneous relationship with: dirt, grass, dandelions, cats and dogs. So it seems, that to heal the child within, we must return to the garden. The Muslim and Christian saints call this transformed state "wakefulness." It is a state of enlightened attention whereby the realities that exist all around us all the time become realities with which we may deepen and enjoy our world. Rumi portrays wakefulness thus:

> The breeze at dawn has secrets to tell you.
> Don't go back to sleep.
>
> You must ask for what you really want.
> Don't go back to sleep. [13]

Rumi, in the most rudimentary language possible, here incisively images wakefulness as a combination of listening to the secrets of nature, and a lucid ability to know what we really want. Sufis have sometimes been called, Searchers for the "Really Real!" This sounds so simple, but to ask "what [we] really want?" can be extremely difficult. We may never have asked this basic question of ourselves, or there may be locked doors in the labyrinth of an unexamined unconscious, hiding the key to our own inner knowing.

What kind of secrets exist in a state of wakefulness? Rumi tells us:

> Let the beauty we love be what we do.
> There are hundreds of ways to
> kneel and kiss the ground.[14]

Enjoying nature is not just a weekend activity, or a one week family vacation. It is a way of being and doing that pervades everyday life. Enjoyment, like praise, is one of the most beneficially healing and naturally occurring states (again, children and beasts can teach us). To bring such a state of creative seeing into our homes and offices, schools and farms, would indeed change us from users into appreciators. There are economic ways[15] to transform and build societies which flourish with the spirituality of the many different religious traditions, and which can motivate us to practice ethical, and thus happier behavior.

> Knowledge alone will not protect nature, nor will ethics, for by themselves they do not arouse motivation strong enough to transform the exploitative patterns to which we have become accustomed. The protection of nature must be rooted in love and delight—in religious experience.[16]

Mystical experiences in nature will give us the endurance to work and change global habits and legislation. In the following true story, we see how powerfully one person's experience and example worked to give us the legacy in the United States, of national parks and preserved wilderness.

In 1903 when John Muir was sixty-five, he was asked by President Theodore Roosevelt, to guide T.R. personally through Yosemite.

> Muir made him a bed of criss-crossed evergreen boughs. "It was clear weather, and we lay in the open." Roosevelt noted, "the enormous cinnamon-colored trunks rising above us like columns of a vaster and more beautiful cathedral than was ever conceived by a human architect."[17]

In 1906 Theodore Roosevelt signed into law Yosemite National Park.

Francis

Probably no saint is associated more with ecology in the west than Francis of Assisi. According to Francis' biographer, Bonaventure, it was because of Francis' close contact with the sacred that made him into such a lover of creation:

> Francis sought occasion to love God in everything. He delighted in all the works of God's hands and from the vision of joy on earth, his mind soared aloft to the life-giving source and cause of all. In everything beautiful, he saw [God] who is beauty itself, and he followed his Beloved everywhere by [God's] likeness imprinted on creation.[18]

Whether the wolf of Gubbio, or the falcon who woke Francis each night to pray, or the lamb that followed the saint into church, Francis had a deep participatory love with all sentient beings. There are plenty of stories about Francis' communication with the created order. Each of these stories demonstrates why so many religious traditions find it easy to relate to this particular Christian saint. Buddhists, Jains, and Muslims, for example, find in Francis, one who really demonstrated his love for all beings.

"Deep calls to deep,"[19] and Francis found the depth of the great artisan even in insects and worms. The stories of Francis removing a worm so that it would not be trampled on the road, or the incident of his freeing doves which had been sold at market, show us just how committed Francis was to these imagers of the divine nature. "He savored in each and every creature— / as in so many rivulets— / that Goodness which is their fountain-source."[20]

Francis even praised the planets and elements as familial: "Brother Sun" and "Sister Moon," "Sister Water" and "Brother Fire." And, of course, "Sister Earth, our mother, who feeds us in her sovereignty and produces various fruits with coloured flowers and herbs."[21]

One of the most beautiful hagiographic stories about Francis which aptly conveys his character, is the story of the Christmas crèche. Francis had a model of the barn where Jesus was born re-created. He had all his close human friends, and all his close animal friends, take their places in this replica of Bethlehem at Greccio. Francis' mirroring of Christ's love for all creation was so real, it was said, that in the manger appeared the Infant Jesus: "This vision was not unfitting for the Child Jesus had been forgotten in the hearts of many; but, by the working of his grace, he was brought to life again through Saint Francis and stamped upon their fervent memory."[22]

The hay in which the Christ child lay was fed to people and animals who were ill, and it freed them from their diseases. "The night was lighted up like the day, and it delighted [people] and beasts. . . The woods rang with the voices of the crowd and the rocks made answer to their jubilation."[23]

The tradition of the crèche has continued all over the world since Francis inaugurated it in the thirteenth century.

Rabi'a

Rabi'a, like so many saints in the various religious traditions, recognized the organic unity between the transcendent and immanent realms. The God who is invisibly present and transcendent is also the God who is visibly immanent and present. All sacredness, whether invisible or visible, is a tribute to Allah, to the glory of the creator, manifested through the abundance of creation. Rabi'a longed to teach of the bond between creator and creation, for she had experienced the essential relationship between transcendence and immanence in her own prayer life and reflections. She gives us a modern ecological theology because of her internal attitude to the creation nourished through her daily encounters with Allah of the near, Allah of unknowability:

> She saw the evidences of God wherever she looked: she never ceased from seeing them all around her. She used to say, in her seclusion: "My Master, through you the ones who loved you came to be near you. For your glory, the mighty whales have praised you in the vast ocean: for your sanctity and holiness the waves have crashed. For you, the darkness of the night and the wheeling stars, the swelling sea, the shining moon, the bright planets: everything you have made in proportion, for you are God the Almighty.[24]

Rabi'a praised God witnessed in whales, stars, and sea; she was in her own way comprehending the Qur'an's words, "whatever is in the heavens and the earth sings the praises of God."[25] She praised God first and foremost in her own being, by living the faith she believed in with her entire will and loving every minute. Secondly, she, as a sentient being, manifested the divine through her actions, striving for peace and the harmonious order Allah had ordained for those who follow and live the clear path: "surely there is peace of heart in the contemplation of

God!"[26] And, thirdly, Rabi'a loved all of life and all sentient creatures because the eye of her mind had been cleansed, and she was able to appreciate the sacred presence in whales, stars, and the sea:

> O God,
> Whenever I listen to the voice of anything You have
>   made—
> The rustling of the trees
> The trickling of water
> The cries of birds
> The flickering of shadow
> The roar of the wind
> The song of the thunder,
>   I hear it saying:
> God is One!
> Nothing can be compared with God![27]

That Rabi'a understood the voice of Being speaking in her own spirit and in the trickling of water, the cries of birds, and the song of thunder, points to the total embodiment of her faith, and why her spirituality is important to contemporary ecology. She was seeing the material universe through a deified vision, and it is that vision which has been lost for the most part, especially in the industrial west: "Nonreligious man has lost the capacity to live religion consciously."[28] Therefore, a religious vision such as Rabi'a's, incorporating an ontological transformation of values, is critical to the recovery of the sacred in relationship to one's own spirituality and justice issues, including the right of the planet and planetary life to exist without the infringement and desecration of violent exploitation.

Rabi'a taught "the balsam and the ointment [needed to heal] the wounded of the Earth."[29] Today the wounded includes the earth herself, immanent Mother. "And in the earth are signs to those of real faith, and in yourselves. What! do you not see?"[30] As in so many traditions, if Islam had been taken more seriously, the immanent message spoken of in the Qur'an, and elaborated by countless Muslim saints, such as Rabi'a, perhaps it would not have been as destructively patriarchal, blind too often to the oppression and cruelty, directed at those usually closer to the immanently divine, namely, women and animals. Rabi'a, by contrast, truly lived a dedicated spirituality of non-harming: "This saint was credited with complete abstinence from animal products so that animals no longer fled from her."[31] Rabi'a included every dimension of life to be deserving of her reverence and respect. The ecological implications of Rabi'a's holiness, are that she sought and found the thread of the sacred in all levels of being and, therein, made no creature unworthy of her love. Allah was revealed in the small and the large; no amount of profit or so-called "progress," justified desecrating holy ground. Rabi'a's unique insight and contribution was that she found that holy ground everywhere.

Afterword

Francis of Assisi lived at the time of the infamous Crusades. In Bonaventure's and Celano's accounts of Francis' life, it is stated that Francis himself had not only a deep longing to go to the Middle East, but wanted to meet the Sultan personally to speak with him on religious matters. Evidently Francis did undertake the extreme hardships of the journey and, according to the historical accounts an encounter with the Sultan did take place. The Sultan was moved by Francis' lack of fear after having been arrested by his armies. The Poverello honestly shared with the Muslim leader his Christian beliefs, and the Sultan listened, finally offering Francis a safe return passage.

Francis' meeting with the Sultan indicates just how long these two great faiths have been attempting to dialogue with each other. There have been centuries when successful breakthroughs in understanding have allowed peace to prosper, and there have been terrible times when hatred and prejudice have ruled the day, leading to bloodshed and misery.

How can we who are the believers of either one of these two magnificent traditions be harbingers of peace? The answer that this book has attempted to present is one that lies at the center of both Islamic and Christian contemplative experience: at the heart of Jesus' and Muhammad's message is a similar truth and transformative path. This is in no way meant to homogenize the individual theological teachings of each faith, or to erase each religion's beautiful practices which are within different ethnic and cultural contexts.

From a contemplative standpoint, however, defining the spiritual journey itself, there are indeed correlations and points of convergence between these two world traditions. Public television had a series on historical personalities from different centuries meeting and speaking with one another at a large seminar table. I would like to ponder what Teresa of Avila might have to share and learn from, for example, Jelaluddin Rumi. Since I have attended numerous interreligious conferences, I have witnessed the value of dialogue as an avenue of understanding and peace. There exists besides dialogue, the advantage of people who share spiritual realities: the willingness to pray, be a part of one another's rituals, music, and scriptural insights. Often what is born from one of these conferences, which now occur worldwide, is a continued willingness among the participants to mobilize in their efforts to establish peace and environmental health.

We do share basic ethical precepts and the stages of the mystical journey. If we are able to respect our differing beliefs and cultures, rather than exaggerate the differences, we may be able to focus on the spiritual and moral similarities which we hold in common.

When it comes to the classical passages leading to union with God, we have seen that some of Christianity's and Islam's most representational mystics speak a language with deep affinities. Indeed, most of what these saints are about has to do with love.

The classical stages themselves grow and flourish because the individual is willing to be transformed and to come closer to God, allowing divine love to enter. The goal of the spiritual journey is union with God, and it is through love that the saints are enabled to endure, find joy in, and pass on the gifts and guidance of the Spirit. We focused, for example, on Rabi'a and Francis, as embodied teachers, role models, who through the specific acts of their lives have displayed a courage and caring for others both human and animal, with which we can still identify in our own time and sociological setting.

Love is the foundation, the ladder, and the circle of the spiritual life. In order to grow in love, most people seem to pass through analogous stages of growth.

The first of these, spiritually, is purification. Purification very often has to do with facing the truth of one's own powerlessness and need for transformation. Only when the individual begins to comprehend what freedom through truth will lead to, in terms of self-esteem, and sharing with others, will the strength be found to help one through the continuing cleansing of one's inner being. Yunus Emre who was quoted earlier, has these powerful lines describing the encounter with the Spirit who is Truth:

> You fall in love with Truth and begin to cry
> You become holy light both inside and out,
> singing Allah, Allah.

You begin to cry because of many reasons. Among them is the fact that one begins to realize just how near God has always been. This is the birth of an awareness of our legitimate ontological status as imagers of the divine. The Spirit's guidance, therefore, corresponds to how identified and willing we are to be and express truth. That is the holy light "both inside and out," which is the basis for another reason to weep (!), namely, the joyous realization that God loves us, and that the entire universe vibrates with divine presence.

If we come back home to the garden wherein all reality sings of God, we discover that interior wisdom unifying our being through the classical mystical stages of divine love. It is the transformed individual who brings peace. Muhammad and Jesus reveal ways to become one with God as the fulfillment of our human nature. They both point to prayer as the vehicle bringing the transformative power of God into our own body-self, personal relationships, attitude toward the planet, work, and commitments to collective social values.

Hopefully, by elucidating, and placing the contemplative stages in the forefront, we may gain the ability to remake ourselves through love and, therein, be participators on the path to peace, and protectors of a qualitative life for our children and the earth.

Notes

1. The Way of Love

1. Charles Upton, *Doorkeeper of the Heart: Versions of Rabi'a* (Putney, Vermont: Threshold Books, 1988), p. 22.
2. John 13:34–35. All quotations are from the Revised Standard Version, 1971 edition, unless otherwise noted.
3. Saint Teresa of Avila, *The Collected Works,* translated by Otilio Rodriguez, OCD, and Kieran Kavanaugh, OCD, Volume II (Washington, D.C.: Institute of Carmelite Studies, 1980), *The Way of Perfection,* Chapter 40, p. 194.
4. Matthew 22:38–39.
5. Fakruddin 'Iraqi.
6. Ibid., *Divine Flashes,* translated by William Chittick and Peter Lamborn Wilson (New York: Paulist Press, 1982), *Flash XVI,* p. 104. The male gender references to God have been changed to terms such as, the One, the Holy One, God. If Islam and Christianity are to continue to speak to people who have judged these two traditions as unfairly patriarchal, language must also express the love of God as free from prejudice and affording equal status to female/male gender through enlightened God-language.
7. Saint John of the Cross, *The Collected Works,* translated by Otilio Rodriguez, OCD, and Kieran Kavanaugh, OCD (Washington D.C.: Institute of Carmelite Studies, 1979), *Romance 2, v. 6,* p. 725.

8. Qur'an, v. 35. See, *The Holy Qur-an,* translated by Abdullah Yusuf Ali (New York: McGregor & Werner, 1946).

9. Ibn 'Abbad of Ronda, *Letters on the Sufi Path,* translated by John Renard (New York: Paulist Press, 1986), *Letter 6:22,* p. 139.

10. Song 2:10–14.

11. See, Mircea Eliade, *The Sacred and the Profane,* translated by Willard R. Trask (New York: Harcourt, Brace, Jovanovich, 1959). One of the best generalized examinations of the effect of secularization on the sacred perception of reality.

12. Jalal al-Din Rumi, *Mystical Poems of Rumi,* translated by A.J. Arberry (Chicago: University of Chicago Press, 1968), p. 8.

13. John 1:14.

14. John 21:12.

15. John 17:25–26.

16. Catherine of Siena, *The Dialogue,* translated by Suzanne Noffke, OP (New York: Paulist Press, 1980), 13:6, p. 50.

17. Ibid., 166:1, p. 363.

18. Qur'an XX:IV:35.

19. Upton, *Doorkeeper,* p. 9.

20. Ibid., pp. 10–11.

21. Idries Shah, *The Sufis,* introduction by Robert Graves (New York: Doubleday, 1971), p. 185.

22. Annemarie Schimmel, *Mystical Dimensions of Islam* (Chapel Hill: University of North Carolina Press, 1986), p. 40.

23. Upton, *Doorkeeper,* p. 30.

24. Saint Bonaventure, *The Life of Saint Francis,* edited and translated by Ewert H. Cousins (New York: Paulist Press, 1978), p. 250.

25. Genesis 3:8.
26. Marion A. Habig, editor, *English Omnibus of the Sources for the Life of St. Francis* (Chicago: Franciscan Herald Press, 1983), *Writings of St. Francis, p. 130.*
27. Ibid., p. 131.

2. The Need for Purification

1. Al-Ghazzali, *Alchemy of Happiness,* quoted in Schimmel's *Mystical Dimensions of Islam,* p. 196.
2. Matthew 5:29–30.
3. Jalal al-Din Rumi, *Open Secret,* translated by John Moyne and Coleman Barks (Vermont: Threshold, 1984), v. 1131.
4. John of the Cross, *Ascent of Mount Carmel,* Book I, Chap. 13, no. 11, pp. 103–104.
5. Rumi, *Open Secret,* v. xi.
6. "Although not a poet by profession, Rumi became a poet of unrivalled dimensions and grandeur after his encounter with Shams al Dīn Tabrīzī. From that day until the last days of his life, Rumi poured forth the profoundest metaphysical truths into the mould of poetry and created some of the most beautiful Persian poetry." Seyyed Hossein Nasr, *Islamic Art and Spirituality* (New York: State University of New York, 1987), p. 127.
7. Rumi, *Open Secret,* p. 42.
8. Philippians 2:5–7; emphasis mine.
9. Cf 1 Kings 19:12.
10. Rumi, *Mystical Poems,* p. 92.
11. Qur'an 11:109 (Arberry translation).
12. John of the Cross, *The Dark Night,* Book II, Chap. 9, no. 3, p. 347.

13. Ibid., *The Living Flame of Love*, v. 2, p. 717.
14. Ḥadīth, Schimmel, *Mystical Dimensions*, p. 190.
15. Nasr, *Islamic Art*, quoting Rumi, p. 128.
16. Shah, *The Sufis*, p. 357.
17. Nasr, *Islamic Art*, quoting Rumi, p. 141.
18. Cf Seyyed Hossein Nasr, *Knowledge and the Sacred* (New York: Crossroad, 1982), pp. 29–30.
19. Nasr, *Islamic Art*, p. 139.
20. Arberry, *Mystical Poems*, 2:8–9, p. 9.
21. Jellaludin Rumi, *Unseen Rain*, translated by John Moyne and Coleman Barks (Vermont: Threshold, 1986), p. 19.
22. Ibid., p. 57.
23. Ibid., p. 56.
24. Ibid., p. 63.
25. Teresa of Avila, *The Interior Castle*, translated by Kieran Kavanaugh, OCD, and Otilio Rodriquez, OCD (New York: Paulist Press, 1979), Chap. II, no. 8, p. 42.
26. Ibid., Raimundo Panikkar, *Preface*, xvii.
27. Ibid., Chap. III, no. 6, p. 51.
28. Ibid., Chap. V, no. 12, p. 72.
29. Ibid.
30. Ibid., Panikkar, *Preface*, xix.
31. Teresa of Avila, *The Collected Works*, Volume II, *Meditations on the Song of Songs*, Chap. 2, no. 2, p. 223.

3. Transformation

1. Rumi, *Dīwāni-i Shams-i Tabrīzī:29958*, translated by William C. Chittick, *The Sufi Path of Love: The Spiritual Teachings of Rumi* (Albany: SUNY Press, 1983), p. 33.
2. Rumi, *Mathnawī VI:1740; The Sufi Path of Love*, p. 55.
3. Ephesians 4:22–24.

4. Bonaventure, *The Soul's Journey into God,* translated by Ewert Cousins (New York: Paulist Press, 1978), p. 99.

5. *The Book of Privy Counseling,* translated by William Johnston (New York: Image Books, 1973), p. 150.

6. Yunnus Emre, *The Drop that Became the Sea,* translated from the Turkish by Kabir Helminski and Refik Algan (Vermont: Threshold, 1989), selected verses from #38, pp. 65–66.

7. Fakhruddin' Iraqi, *Divine Flashes, XXV,* p. 120.

8. Mark 6:50.

9. Shah, *The Sufis,* p. 11.

10. Bonaventure, *The Life of St. Francis,* Chap. 8, p. 250.

11. Ibid., p. 261.

12. 'Attar's poem *the Human Case,* in *The Drunken Universe,* translated by P. Wilson and N. Poujavady (Michigan: Phanes, 1987), p. 22.

13. Rumi, *Open Secret,* p. 80.

14. Bonaventure, *The Soul's Journey into God,* p. 77.

15. Ibid.

16. Qur'an, translated by Kenneth Cragg (London: Collins Liturgical Publications, 1990), *Surah 10:5–6;* p. 100.

17. Thomas Merton, *New Seeds of Contemplation,* p. 13.

18. William Johnston, editor, *The Cloud of Unknowing* (New York: Doubleday, 1973), p. 80.

19. Rumi, *Open Secret,* p. 81.

20. Merton, *New Seeds,* p. 100.

21. Chittick, *The Sufi Path,* p. 39.

22. Rabi'a, *Doorkeeper, #56,* p. 46.

23. 1 Timothy 1:5.

24. John 18:37.

25. See Schimmel, *Mystical Dimensions,* pp. 64, 66, etc.

26. John 18:37.

27. Rumi, *This Longing,* translated by C. Barks and J.

Moyne (Vermont: Threshold, 1988), *Mathnawi V: 2211–2220,* p. 45.

28. Emre, *The Drop, #42,* p. 72.
29. Isaiah 11:6.
30. Matthew 18:3–4.
31. Meister Eckhart, *The Essential Sermons, Commentaries, Treatises, and Defense,* translated by E. Colledge and B. McGinn (New York: Paulist Press, 1981), p. 31.
32. Ibid., *Counsel 6,* p. 254.
33. Rumi, *These Branching Moments,* translated by C. Barks and J. Moyne (Brown University: Copper Beech Press, 1988), p. 3.
34. Qur'an 31:28, Chittick's translation, *The Sufi Path,* p. 72.
35. Ibid., Qur'an 108:1.

4. Union

1. Shāh Ne'matollāh, quoted in *The Drunken Universe,* p. 96.
2. Herbert Mason, *The Death of al-Hallaj* (Notre Dame: The University of Notre Dame, 1979), p. 20.
3. Mark 1:40–42.
4. Yunus Emre, quoted in *Islamic Spirituality: Manifestation,* edited by Seyyed Hossein Nasr (New York: Crossroad, 1991), p. 352.
5. *The Cloud of Unknowing,* Johnston, Chap. 20, p. 75.
6. Ibid., Chap. 17, p. 71.
7. John of the Cross, *Stanzas Concerning an Ecstasy Experienced in High Contemplation,* in *The Collected Works, #7,* p. 719.
8. Ibid., *The Dark Night, #5,* p. 711.
9. Rumi, *This Longing,* p. 59.

10. Hafiz of Shiraz, *News of Love, Versions* by David Cloutier (Greensboro: Unicorn, 1984), p. 4.

11. We do not have the space here to dwell on factors such as patriarchy's attitudes toward the "earthly" in regard to women and nature. Nor, dwell on the modern exaggeration of so trying to rebalance the present spiritual outlook with earthly spirituality, that the heavenly is disregarded.

    Needless to say, both dimensions have to be continually reexamined in the light of their authentic religious bases: Muhammad's and Jesus' own embodied teachings. These reflect the tradition's intuitive understanding of aiding each human being in integrating the earthly and heavenly, whether this be in her own life, or in the expression of the tradition's credos and communal actions.

12. John Ruusbroec, *The Spiritual Espousals and Other Works,* translated by James Wiseman (New York: Paulist Press, 1985), p. 117.

13. Rabi'a, *Doorkeeper of the Heart,* #53, p. 45.

14. Rumi, *The Sufi Path of Love,* p. 186.

5. A God-Centered Ecology

1. Genesis 1:31.

2. John of the Cross, *Spiritual Canticle,* in *The Collected Works,* #14 and #15, p. 412.

3. Sa'd ud Din Mahmūd Shabistarī, *The Secret Rose Garden,* translated by Florence Lederer (Michigan: Phanes Press, 1987), *The Name,* p. 72.

4. Qur'an 17:44.

5. Job 12:7–10.

6. Psalm 139:13, 15.
7. Genesis 9:2. Cf the excellent essay by William Dyrness, "Stewardship of the Earth in the Old Testament," in *Tending the Garden,* edited by Wesley Granberg-Michaelson (Michigan: William B. Eerdmans, 1987).
8. Ibid., Essay by Robert K. Johnson, "Wisdom Literature and Its Contribution to a Biblical Environmental Ethic," p. 69.
9. Hosea 2:18.
10. Mark 4:30–32.
11. Seyyed Hossein Nasr, *Islamic Art and Spirituality* (New York: State University of New York, 1987), p. 11.
12. "Omnis mundi creatura quasi liber et pictura nobis est et speculum." Alanus de Insulis in his *De Incarnatione Christi* (twelfth century).
13. Rumi, *Open Secret,* #91.
14. Ibid., #82.
15. To transform our modern world into a wholistic and healthy society seems eminently practical. Even now there are businesses that are attempting to change their orientation from destroyers to preservers of the earth. Some think this sort of change is merely an attempt to evade environmental legislation, but this is a moot point.

   An example of jobs being created through a changed attitude is in the cattle industry. Some ranches have been converted into farms which produce profitable crops such as grain. This will at least cut down on air and river pollution which is created by manure. Furthermore, it will decrease the human consumption of the cattle's flesh containing hormones and antibiotics and eliminate factory farming which would horrify the most cold-blooded carnivore.

Important books to read on this subject are *Diet for a Small Planet,* by Francis Morre Lappé, and *Diet for a New America,* by John Robbins.

16. Richard Cartwright Austin, *Baptized into Wilderness: A Christian Perspective on John Muir* (Atlanta: John Knox Press, 1984), p. 3. An inspiring book.

17. Ibid., p. 69.

18. Bonaventure, *Major Life, Omnibus IX:1,* p. 698.

19. Psalm 42:7.

20. Bonaventure, *The Life of St. Francis,* IX:1, p. 263.

21. This stanza on "Sister Earth" bears repeating from *Chapter I. The Canticle of Brother Sun, Omnibus,* pp. 130–131.

22. Celano, *First Life, Omnibus,* 86, p. 301.

23. Ibid., pp. 85–86, 300–301. Cf to the bleak portrait of Marjorie Spiegel's, *The Dreaded Comparison: Human and Animal Slavery,* with a Preface by Alice Walker.

    Walker states: "The animals of the world exist for their own reasons. They were not made for humans any more than black people were made for whites or women for men."

    The book begins with a poem entitled "Sympathy" by Paul Laurence Dunbar, son of two runaway slaves. The last verse reads: "I know why the caged bird sings!"

24. Ibid., pp. 82–83.

25. Qur'an 59:1.

26. Qur'an 13:28.

27. Upton, *Doorkeeper,* p. 48.

28. Mircea Eliade, *The Sacred and the Profane: The Nature of Religion,* translated by Willard R. Trask (New York: Harcourt Brace Jovanovich, 1959), p. 213.

29. Widad El Sakkakini, *First Among Sufis: The Life and Thought of Rabi'a al-Adawiyya,* translated by Nabil Saf-

wat, with an Introduction by Doris Lessing (London: Octagon Press, 1982), p. 83.

30. Qur'an 51:20–21. Cf Al-Hafiz Masri, *Animals in Islam* (England: The Athene Trust, 1989): "Islam wants us to think and act in positive terms of accepting all species as communities like us in their own right and not to sit in judgement on them according to our human norms and values." P. vii.

Index